SALVATION

God's Full Salvation

A LESSON BOOK - LEVEL ONE

*Based on and Compiled from
the Writings of*

WATCHMAN NEE
AND
WITNESS LEE

Living Stream Ministry
Anaheim, CA • www.lsm.org

First Edition, June 1990.

ISBN 978-0-87083-521-6

Published by

Living Stream Ministry
2431 W. La Palma Ave., Anaheim, CA 92801 U.S.A.
P. O. Box 2121, Anaheim, CA 92814 U.S.A.

Printed in the United States of America

13   14   15   16   17   18   /   12   11   10   9   8   7

TABLE OF CONTENTS

INTRODUCTION
TO THE LESSON BOOK

Concerning the Lesson Books

This lesson book is one in a series originally designed to teach the truth to junior high and high school students during their summer school of the truth. Because the lesson books were written over a period of several years, the books may vary in style and format.

Concerning This Lesson Book

This is the first lesson book in this series. This book is based upon and compiled from the writings of Brother Watchman Nee and Brother Witness Lee.

Throughout history many Christians have given themselves to study the Word of God. The Lord has always blessed those who enjoy and share with others the rich truths that are found in the Bible. Christians must be those who love God's Word and continually seek to know the truth that it contains. The more points of the truth we see, the more we shall be able to experience the Lord.

Studying the Bible, however, is not always so simple. The Bible has many pages that tell us about countless different things. You probably have experienced getting lost sometimes while trying to read it. This is one of the reasons why this lesson book has been written. It will help you to see clearly what the Bible tells us about God's full salvation. Each lesson presents an important truth concerning salvation.

There is more than enough truth in this book for you to go over each lesson many times. We encourage you to use these lessons at home with your family and friends as well. You will find that studying the truth with others can be most enjoyable. If you are faithful to study and understand these truths, your love and appreciation for the Lord should grow tremendously. You will realize that God's salvation is extremely full, very complete.

To be able to know the truth concerning full salvation as a young person is a tremendous privilege which you should not take lightly. It is also a great responsibility. The future of the Lord's recovery depends upon the young people being trained in the proper knowledge of the truths revealed in the Bible. We hope that you would give yourselves to be equipped in that way. We believe this lesson book will be a helpful and enjoyable way to receive such training.

The Structure of the Lessons

The title conveys the subject of the lesson. The verses are for reading or pray-reading. The outline gives you an overview of the lesson. It is good to read the outline first to get an overview of the lesson before you proceed to the text of the lesson. The text is organized according to the outline. The writing contained inside the brackets [ ] are quotes from Brother Nee's and Brother Lee's publications. The questions are intended to help you better understand and apprehend the lesson. A list of books with the author, publisher, and page number is included for all quoted materials. Finally, a list of books is included for further reference on the subject of each lesson. Nee represents Brother Nee. Lee represents Brother Witness Lee. LSM represents Living Stream Ministry. HKCBR represents Hong Kong Church Book Room.

The Versions Used in Quotes

When quoting verses, we used the American Standard Version of the Bible for the Old Testament and the Recovery Version of the Bible for the New Testament. We sometimes replaced New Testament quotations found inside the brackets [ ] with the corresponding Recovery Version verse.

The Proper Attitude Needed to Study the Word with the Help of the Lesson Book

This lesson book is not the Bible. It is a lesson book based on the Bible. It can be used as a study aid for the Bible. Do not quote the lesson book as the authoritative source for biblical truths or teachings. You must learn to reference the appropriate source—which book, which chapter, and which verse, etc. You must also learn how all the key verses relate to one another in presenting the vision of the church and the way to build up the church. Take the time to know the Word of God with certainty.

The Way to Study the Word
with This Lesson Book

The Word of God embodies the essence of the Spirit. Therefore, when you come to the Word, you must use your spirit. The best way to use your spirit is to pray. You must pray before, during, and after the studying of this lesson book. It is also important that you fellowship as you are studying. It is not adequate to read by yourself without fellowshipping with others. The fellowship of the Body is necessary to help you comprehend the heavenly vision.

Suggestions on the Summer School of the Truth

It is suggested that the summer school of the truth be six weeks in length. Each week should be divided into four days, each day lasting three hours. Twenty-four days, each with three hours, will provide adequate time to pray, to cover all the lessons, and to fellowship. We recommend that all the students practice to write prophecies for each lesson, and also practice prophesying to speak for Christ and speak forth Christ. Each student should endeavor to experience individually and corporately what he has learned.

We have prayed and will continue to pray for you, that you may have an enjoyable time together during your summer school of the truth, that you will progress towards the full knowledge of the truth, and be built up in your locality. Amen!

June 1990   Paul Hon
Pleasant Hill, California

Lesson One

SALVATION IN GOD'S PLAN

Scripture Reading

Eph. 3:9-11; 1:9-11; 1 Tim. 1:4; Eph. 3:2; Gen. 1:26

Outline

I. God's plan in eternity past
II. God's good pleasure
III. God's eternal purpose
IV God's economy
V. God's enemy
VI. God's salvation

Text

This lesson book covers the subject of God's full salvation. What does God's full salvation mean? Why do we need to be saved? From what and into what are we saved? Why does God want to save us and why can He alone save us? How does He save us and what do we have to do to be saved? This is a long list of questions to consider. This book will answer all these questions and tell you more about God's salvation. In this first lesson we want to cover something that you might never have heard before, something that happened in eternity past.

I. GOD'S PLAN IN ETERNITY PAST

The book of Ephesians tells us that before God created anything, when He was all alone, He had a good pleasure, a heart's desire. According to this good pleasure, He made a plan, a will. The Bible calls this "the purpose of the ages," or "the eternal purpose" (Eph. 3:11). God also made an arrangement or a way by which He could fulfill this eternal purpose. The Bible calls this arrangement God's economy or God's dispensation (1 Tim. 1:4; Eph. 1:10; 3:2). So, the Bible reveals to us that in eternity past God had an eternal purpose according to His good pleasure and an economy or a means to fulfill that purpose.

II. GOD'S GOOD PLEASURE

What is God's good pleasure? It is simply what pleases Him and makes Him happy. All that God has done has been according to this good pleasure, just as you and I do things according to what pleases us and makes us happy.

III. GOD'S ETERNAL PURPOSE

What is God's eternal purpose which is according to His good pleasure? God's eternal purpose is to have a group of people, a corporate man, created in His image and likeness. God desires this man to be filled with Him as life in order to express Him and have His dominion to represent Him. This is God's eternal purpose because it was planned by God before time began and will never change.

IV. GOD'S ECONOMY

And what is God's economy or His way to fulfill this purpose? God's way to gain such a corporate man is by dispensing Himself into man as life. Without dispensing Himself into man, His purpose can never be accomplished.

V. GOD'S ENEMY

But, before He could do so, Satan, God's enemy, came in to deceive man and to inject his own sinful life and nature into man. Through this, man fell into a pitiful condition, full of sinful acts and a sinful nature which ruined him for God's great purpose.

VI. GOD'S SALVATION

God, however, cannot be defeated! Though man fell and God's plan was frustrated, God still loved man and would not be moved from His purpose. So, God took action to save man in order to accomplish His eternal purpose. This action is His full salvation.

Questions

1. What is God's "good pleasure"?

2. Give an illustration from your own life to explain what the Bible means by God's good pleasure, His purpose, and His economy.

3. What is God's eternal purpose?

4. Define the word "eternal."

5. Why do we say that God's purpose is eternal?

6. Define the word "economy." What is God's economy?

Further Reference

See Compendium of God's Full Salvation (LSM), Chapter 1, I. A.

or

1. Life-study of First Corinthians (Lee/LSM), p. 96.

2. Life-study of Ephesians (Lee/LSM), pp. 631-632.

3. The Completing Ministry of Paul (Lee/LSM), p. 9.

Lesson Two

GOD SELECTED AND PREDESTINATED MANY PEOPLE TO BE HIS SONS

Scripture Reading

Eph. 1:4-5; Rom. 9:11-13; 8:29; John 8:44; 1:12

Outline

I. God's selection
II. God's predestination
III. Sonship—the goal of God's selection

Text

I. GOD'S SELECTION

To fulfill His eternal purpose, God needed to create man. But even before this, He had to choose or select some of them from among billions to be His sons. So, before God created anything, He selected certain ones. You may wonder how we know this. Well, the Bible tells us so in Ephesians 1:4, "According as He chose us in Him before the foundation of the world that we should be holy and without blemish before Him, in love."

You then may ask, "Why did He choose me and not some-one else?" He chose you because He wanted to, because it was His good pleasure to do so, not according to how good or capable you are. This verse also tells us that He chose us in Christ, "in Him," not for what we were in ourselves.

According to what the Bible calls His "foreknowledge," God knew when, where and of whom we would be born. Romans 9:11 illustrates this with the story of Jacob. Before Jacob was born, before he had a chance to do good or bad, God chose him and not his brother Esau. It was the same with us. Isn't this wonderful? This selection by God is His first bless-ing to us, and we should all thank Him very much for it.

II. GOD'S PREDESTINATION

After He chose us, God "predestinated" us to be His sons. "Predestinate" means "to mark out beforehand or ahead of time unto a certain purpose." Before God created us, He put His mark upon us to show that we were His. Can you see any "mark" on you? No, certainly not; but God can, and Satan can too. God knows, Satan knows, and even the angels know that we are the ones chosen and marked out ahead of time by God to contain God and express Him as sons. In our experience, this means that whether or not we care to become His sons, He will still have His way with us and bring us all the way to His goal.

III. SONSHIP—THE GOAL OF GOD'S SELECTION

The goal of God's selection and predestination is "sonship." In the Bible, this word means two main things: maturity in God's life and the position to inherit all that God is. A child has his father's life, but because he is not full-grown, he cannot inherit all that his father may have to give to him. He can receive the inheritance only when he is full-grown, when he is mature. It is just the same with us. God has chosen us to be His sons, full of the divine life and matured. You may have the Father's divine life, which makes you His child. But God has chosen and predestinated you not just to be his child, but eventually to be His son, one who is fully matured in His divine life. Only when you become such a person can you be qualified to inherit all that He is and has done for you. We need to thank Him for choosing us and we need to receive His life. This will enable us to become His many sons to grow up into Him and express Him (John 1:12).

After the fall of man, the whole human race became sinners, the sons of the Devil (John 8:44). But God chose us to become His sons. How wonderful! Although we don't look much like Him today, we have confidence in His selection that one day we will be the many full-grown sons of God, full of His life to express Him and full of His dominion to represent Him. This one expression of God is the church today, the Body of Christ, and will be the New Jerusalem in the future.

Questions

1. In His full salvation, God has blessed us with many things. What is the first great blessing of His salvation?

2. When did God select us and predestinate us, and how?

3. What is the difference between God's selection and His predestination?

4. God has selected us and predestinated us, but can we reject Him? What then shall we do?

5. What is the goal of God's selection?

6. What is the biblical meaning of "sonship"?

7. How can a person become a son of God?

Further References

See Compendium of God's Full Salvation (LSM),
Chapter 1, I. B. 1.

or

1. Life-study of Ephesians (Lee/LSM), pp. 597-598, 635-636.

2. Life-study of Galatians (Lee/LSM), pp. 248-249, 399-400.

Lesson Three

GOD'S GOAL—A CORPORATE MAN

Scripture Reading

Eph. 3:9-11; 1:22-23; 2:10, 19-22

Outline

I. The church—the Body of Christ
II. God's masterpiece

Text

Before we go any further, we need to see something of great importance to our understanding of God's full salvation. The goal of God's salvation is not many individual people who have been saved by God, but one corporate man. What is a corporate man? Men, as we know them, are all individuals, independent from one another. How can there be such a thing as a corporate man?

I. THE CHURCH—THE BODY OF CHRIST

As we saw in the last lesson, the sons of God all have God's life. Actually, God's life is not a thing but a Person, God Himself. To have this life is just to have a living Person in us, the living God Himself. When these many individual people become filled with the one living God, they become one corporate God-man. They are no longer many individuals. They have all become the many parts of this one corporate man, the many members of the Body of Christ.

Consider yourself. Inside your body you have only one life, one person living there. When you go to school, your whole person goes. When you do a job, your whole person does the job. All that you do, you do in oneness, because within you there are not two persons but only one.

How about God? He too is in oneness, and His purpose is to be expressed in this oneness. When so many individual people receive Him as life, they become one with Him, and they are called the church, the Body of Christ. In eternity future, these people will be called the New Jerusalem. This is what we call the corporate man that God desires. This is what makes God happy.

If you read Ephesians 3:9-11, you will see that the church is not a thing that just happened after many individual people were saved. No! Rather, the church was planned in eternity past. It was for the church that the many people were saved. It was planned in eternity past. Then, in time, through our salvation in Christ, the church was brought about to express God. According to Revelation 21 and 22, it will continue on into eternity as the eternal goal and dwelling place of God.

What is the church? The church is a people filled up with God as their life. They are no more just individuals who care for their own things. Instead, they are many individuals who are being filled up with God as their life and are being built up together in Him. When they are living in this one life, they have the one image of God. They are His one expression and they represent God with His authority.

II. GOD'S MASTERPIECE

In all of God's creation, this corporate man, the church, is the most marvelous of all God's works. Ephesians 2:10 tells us that the church is God's "masterpiece." Not even the heavens with all of its marvels, nor the earth with all of its beauty, can compare with the church. The church is God's unique desire. It is His purpose from eternity, and it is the product of His economy—His heart's desire.

Questions

1. What is the meaning of "one corporate man"? How is it possible for so many individual people to become this?

2. Which verses in Ephesians tell us that the church did not just happen after so many people were saved but was instead according to His eternal plan?

3. Compare what most people think of when they hear the word "church" with the church as it is revealed in Ephesians. Do the two views have anything in common?

Further Reference

See Compendium of God's Full Salvation (LSM), Chapter 1, I. B. 2.

or

1. The Practical Expression of the Church (Lee/LSM), pp. 7-8.

2. Life-study of Ephesians (Lee/LSM), pp. 495, 624-630.

3. Life-study of Genesis (Lee/LSM), pp. 472-473.

4. Life-study of Exodus (Lee/LSM), pp. 633, 1326.

5. Life-study of Second Corinthians (Lee/LSM), p. 374.

6. Life-study of Revelation (Lee/LSM), pp. 27-28.

7. The Divine Dispensing of the Divine Trinity (Lee/LSM), pp. 13-14.

Lesson Four

GOD'S CREATION OF MAN AS A THREE-PART VESSEL

Scripture Reading

Gen. 1:26; Rom. 9:21-23; 1 Thes. 5:23; Gen. 2:7; Matt. 22:37; Eph. 3:16; 1 Pet. 3:4; John 3:6

Outline

I. Man in God's image and likeness
II. Man—a vessel to contain God
   A. The body
   B. The soul
   C. The spirit

Text

In Lesson One we saw God's marvelous eternal plan. In Lesson Two we saw the selection of the people to fulfill His plan. According to this plan and selection, God then went ahead to create the heavens and the earth for man. Finally, He created man, the center of His creation, in a very special way.

I. MAN IN GOD'S IMAGE AND LIKENESS

First, in Genesis 1:26, God said, "Let us make man in our image, after our likeness." Here we can see that God created man differently from all other creatures. All the other things that God created were after their own kind. Only man was after God's kind. Do you see how close man is to God? A good way to illustrate how man is in God's image is with a glove and a hand. Man is to God like a glove is to a hand. A glove is made according to the shape of a hand and for the hand to enter into the glove. Man was created according to God's image and after His likeness so that God could enter into him. Do you see how wonderful you are? Only you, among all of God's creation, were made in such a wonderful way. This makes you a "V.I.P." of the universe. You were created as a vessel in the image of God so that you could contain Him and express Him. None of this was by accident or evolution. It was absolutely planned by God in eternity past and carried out in His creation for the fulfillment of His eternal purpose.

II. MAN—A VESSEL TO CONTAIN GOD

Second, the Bible tells us that God created man in His image and likeness as a vessel (Rom. 9:21-23). The purpose of a vessel is to contain something. A bottle may contain something to drink. That is its function or purpose. Man was made to contain God. That is his function or purpose.

However, we are not simple vessels, but vessels of three parts: spirit, soul and body (1 Thes. 5:23). So, we call man a "tripartite" vessel or being.

A. The Body

The first part of man is his body, the physical part. It was created by God from the dust of the ground (Gen. 2:7). Through our physical body, we can live on the earth. We can touch, see, smell and hear things with our body. As you are reading this lesson, you are using your hands to hold the book and your eyes to read it.

B. The Soul

The soul is the psychological part of man. This is you, your person or your personality, and it has three parts or organs: your mind, your emotion and your will. As you are trying to understand this lesson, you are using the organ of your mind. You may get excited about being a man created in God's image and want to know more. This is your emotion being stirred up. And as you determine to read the Bible to find out more about God and man, you are using your will to make a decision. The soul is the part of man created by God for us to know Him, love Him and turn to Him so we can be saturated with God and express Him.

C. The Spirit

The spirit is the deepest part of man. The Bible calls it "the inner man" (Eph. 3:16) and "the hidden man of the heart" (1 Pet. 3:4) because it is deeper and harder to know than our other two parts. Of all God's creatures, only man was created with a spirit. Its function is to contact God and to receive Him. Did you know that you not only have a body and a soul but a spirit too? You may never have considered it. If you have never come to God, you have never had to use your spirit. You need your body and soul to exist as a human, but if you have never come to God, you have never used your spirit. Just as our ears are for hearing sound and our eyes are for seeing colors, our spirit is the organ for receiving God's life and for being one with Him. Hallelujah! What a wonderful spirit God has made within us! With our spirit, we can contact God and contain Him to express Him on the earth. This is exactly what makes God happy and fulfills His eternal purpose in creating man.

Do you have any friends who do not know the Lord or who say that He doesn't exist? This is because they have never used their spirit to contact God. They are like a blind man who does not believe in colors because he has never seen them. In the same way, some men do not believe in God because they have never used their spirit to contact Him.

As for you, you may know how to use your body very well and how to take care of it properly. You are also going to school to train your mind to know many things and to function properly. But, to be someone fully according to God's purpose, you also need to learn how to use your spirit to contact God, to receive Him and to contain Him.

Questions

1. In what two ways is man different from all other creatures that God made?

2. Romans 9 tells us that God made man a vessel. Why does the Bible describe man in this way?

3. List the three parts of man and their functions. Give examples of how you use each part.

4. Write a list of seven things you can find around your house that are containers and alongside that write down their contents.

5. How does this illustrate the fact that man is God's vessel, His container?

Further Reference

See Compendium of God's Full Salvation (LSM), Chapter 1, II.

or

1. Life-study of John (Lee/LSM), p. 59.

2. Life-study of Genesis (Lee/LSM), pp. 62-64, 67, 129-131.

3. Life-study of Romans (Lee/LSM), pp. 656-658.

4. Life-study of Galatians (Lee/LSM), pp. 401-402.

5. The Glorious Church (Nee/LSM), pp. 8-9.

Lesson Five

THE TREE OF LIFE
AND THE RIVER
SIGNIFYING GOD AS LIFE TO MAN

Scripture Reading

Gen. 2:9-10; John 1:4; 14:6; 10:10; 6:57; 7:37-38; Rev. 22:1

Outline

I. Man placed in the garden of Eden
II. The tree of life in the garden's center
III. Life needed for God's expression
IV. The tree of life signifying Christ
V. The river of life quenching our thirst

Text

I. MAN PLACED IN THE GARDEN OF EDEN

After God created man, He planted a beautiful garden and put the man there. In the garden there were many fruit trees good for food. In the center of the garden was the tree of life and with it a river. It was in front of this tree that God put the man.

At that time, what was the most important need of man? Did he need a job to earn money in order to eat? No, all that he needed for living had been provided for him by God. Did God tell the man to do good and to be a good person? No, He simply created him and then put him in front of the tree of life in the garden. To realize what man needed most, you must remember what God's purpose was in creating man. He was not created to make a living or to be good and do good; he was created to express God in His image by being filled up with His life. So, what man needed the most was for God to be his life.

II. THE TREE OF LIFE
IN THE GARDEN'S CENTER

You have heard about the garden of Eden, but do you know what was the most outstanding feature in the garden? You may think it was its beauty or pleasantness, but this was not so. The most outstanding feature was the tree of life at the center. This tree signified God as life to man. The garden of Eden was not just a beautiful place, but a place where man could receive God as life and be filled with God in order to fulfill God's eternal purpose and satisfy God.

III. LIFE NEEDED FOR GOD'S EXPRESSION

Even though God had created man in His image and according to His likeness, it was impossible for this man to express God without receiving Him as life. Simply to have the outward form of God's image and authority was not enough. For man to express God and represent Him, he needed God's life. Without God's life, we are utterly unable and unqualified to express God and represent Him. A light bulb is a good illustration. It is made to express electricity by shining, but if electricity never comes into it, it can never fulfill its function. It is just the same with man. Man is a "light bulb" to express God, the divine light. But to do this, the divine electricity, God's life, must come into man. Though he has been made in God's image and likeness to express Him, man still needs God's life to come into him before he can truly express God.

IV. THE TREE OF LIFE SIGNIFYING CHRIST

Now, let us turn to Genesis 2:9-10. After God created man, He did not tell man to do good or to do something for Him in order to express Him. Rather, He placed man in front of the tree of life so that man could partake of Him as life. The way he would take God as life into him was by eating Him. The New Testament tells us that this tree of life signifies God incarnated in Christ. John 1:4 tells us that "In Him was life." In John 14:6, the Lord Jesus said that He is "the way, and the reality, and the life." In John 10:10, He told us that He came that we "may have life and may have it abundantly." In John 6:57, the Lord Jesus told us to eat Him. These verses point out that Jesus Christ Himself is the life for man, as portrayed by the tree of life. Isn't this wonderful? Jesus did not come to give us some laws by which we should live. He didn't come to give us a better job, house or car. Instead, He came just to give Himself to us to be our life.

V. THE RIVER OF LIFE QUENCHING OUR THIRST

In the garden there was not only a tree, signifying Christ as our life, but also a river. In Genesis it does not say "a river of life," but in Revelation 22:1 it says, "And he showed me a river of water of life." This river is seen throughout the entire Bible. It signifies God as the Spirit reaching us as life and quenching our thirst. In John 7:37 the Lord Jesus said, "If anyone thirst, let him come to Me and drink." This verse shows that Jesus came to be life to man in the same way that water quenches our thirst. Sometimes, you may feel that nothing is able to satisfy you. That was the case with the people in John 7 (see John 7:37-38). They did not know God's purpose in creating them, nor did they realize their need to take God into them as life. Even though they had just finished a big feast which lasted all week, they were still hungry and thirsty for something more. It was then that Jesus offered Himself to them to be a satisfying drink, bringing God as life to them so that both they and God could be satisfied.

Today, God is still offering Himself to all of us. We all need to come to Him and drink.

Questions

1. When God put man in front of the tree of life in the garden of Eden, what did this signify?

2. Why can we say that man did not need to earn a living or do good to fulfill God's purpose in creating him?

3. Try to explain why man needs God's life as well as His image to be able to express Him. You may use an illustration if you need to.

4. What verses in the New Testament show us that the Lord
    Jesus is the tree of life to man?

5. What does man need the most today?

6. How can we eat the tree of life and drink the river of life
    today?

Further Reference

See Compendium of God's Full Salvation (LSM),
Chapter 1, III. A.

or

1. The Stream (Lee/LSM), vol. 4, no. 2, p. 6.

2. The Kingdom (Lee/LSM), pp. 63-64.

3. Life-study of Genesis (Lee/LSM), pp. 140-142, 146.

Lesson Six

THE FALL OF MAN

Scripture Reading

Gen. 2:9-10, 17; 3:1-6; 1 Tim. 2:14; Rom. 5:18-19

Outline

I. The two trees
   A. Dependence and independence
   B. Life and death
II. Satan—the enemy of God
III. Satan deceives man
IV. The tragedy of the universe
V. Two great problems
   A. Objective
   B. Subjective
VI. Illustration

Text

I. THE TWO TREES

In the last lesson, you may have noticed in Genesis 2:9 that there was another tree besides the tree of life. That tree was the tree of knowledge of good and evil. By eating it, man fell and was completely ruined for God's purpose. In this lesson, we will learn more about these two trees, how man was deceived to eat of the tree of knowledge, and what was the result.

A. Dependence and Independence

The tree of life and the tree of knowledge represent two principles in man's relationship with God. The principle of the tree of life is dependency upon God. To have God as life makes man dependent on God. The principle of the tree of knowledge is independence from God. When we do not take

God as our life, but choose to live according to knowledge instead, we live independently from God and are not able to be filled with Him and express Him as He has planned.

B. Life and Death

While the tree of life represents God's life or God as life to man, the tree of knowledge represents Satan as the source of death. In Genesis 2:17, God told the man that in the day that he ate of the tree of knowledge he would surely die. This shows that the tree of knowledge of good and evil is actually the tree of death. By taking in the tree of knowledge, man took in the element and nature of Satan, which is the source of death.

II. SATAN—THE ENEMY OF GOD

In the Bible, we are shown that Satan was originally Lucifer, the archangel of God. Lucifer means "daystar" or "morning star." Among all God's creatures at that time, he was the most beautiful and wise. Because of this, he aspired to be on the same level as God and independent from God. He wanted God's creatures to worship him. For this reason, he rebelled against God and became God's enemy, always seeking to exalt himself to be equal with God and to frustrate God's purpose.

III. SATAN DECEIVES MAN

Before man could take in God's life, Satan came to Eve, Adam's wife, tempting her to eat of the tree of knowledge. He did this by injecting his own devilish thought into her mind. Satan caused Eve to question God, His word, and His intention. Satan deceived the woman into thinking that she could be independent from God and even become like God. As a result of her being deceived, Eve took of the fruit and ate it, and gave some to her husband, who also ate.

IV. THE TRAGEDY OF THE UNIVERSE

This action of man is the greatest tragedy in the universe. The man God had created to contain and express Him as life disobeyed Him and received the satanic life instead. Now, rather than expressing God, the man created by God would express the sinful life and nature of God's enemy, Satan. As a result of this tragic act, man fell away from God's original intent and purpose. We call this act and its result the fall of man.

V. TWO GREAT PROBLEMS

A. Objective

This action caused two major problems for man. First, on the objective side, man transgressed against God's righteousness by disobeying His commandment to not eat of the tree of knowledge. As a result, man came under God's judgment and lost his right to the tree of life. Rather than being filled with God, he was separated from God. Eventually, he would die in his sins and face God's judgment and the lake of fire after death.

B. Subjective

On the subjective side, man took in the satanic life and that life became a poison in him, constituting him a sinner with a sinful nature. The man God loved so much and had created to be His unique container and expression had been completely ruined by this sinful act.

This great tragedy is man's history. It happened about 6,000 years ago, but its effects on man can be seen today. Having taken of the tree of knowledge and having chosen to be independent from God, man has fallen from God's purpose into a life which is full of sins and constituted with the satanic nature. He is completely ignorant of God and His purpose with man.

VI. ILLUSTRATION

We can illustrate these two problems in this way. A child told by his mother not to drink from a bottle of poison disobeys his mother and drinks from it. He has not only disobeyed his mother and gotten into trouble with her, but much more than that, he has taken poison into him and will die unless something can be done.

By eating of the tree of knowledge, man not only disobeyed God and came under His condemnation. He also took into him the poisonous nature of Satan. In His salvation, God has to take care of both the problem of man's disobedience and the problem of the poisonous, sinful life of Satan which he has taken into him. If He does not do something, man will die in his sins; he will be condemned by God and will be of no use to Him for His eternal purpose.

Questions

1. What do the tree of life and the tree of knowledge signify to man?

2. How did Satan deceive the woman to take of the tree of knowledge? For the answer, you will need to read Genesis 3:1-6.

3. What were the two main results of the fall of man? Use the illustration presented to explain.

4. How do we take of the tree of life or the tree of knowledge? You may need to discuss this with the teacher.

Further Reference

See Compendium of God's Full Salvation (LSM), Chapter 2.

or

1. Life-study of Genesis (Lee/LSM), pp. 14-17, 167, 282-283.

2. Life-study of Romans (Lee/LSM), pp. 115, 117, 371-372, 415, 511.

3. The Glorious Church (Nee/LSM), pp. 10, 18-20.

4. Life-study of Ephesians (Lee/LSM), pp. 83, 270.

5. The Experience of Life (Lee/LSM), pp. 235-236.

6. The Economy of God (Lee/LSM), p. 107.

7. The Kingdom (Lee/LSM), pp. 65-66.

8. Life-study of Exodus (Lee/LSM), pp. 1027-1028.

MAN'S NEED OF SALVATION

Scripture Reading

Rom. 5:18; John 3:36; Heb. 9:27; Matt. 25:41;
Rev. 20:15; Eph. 2:1-2; 4:17-18a; 2 Tim. 3:2-4;
Rom. 7:17-18a; 6:6b; 7:24; John 8:44

Outline

I. The objective problem before God
    A. Under God's condemnation
    B. Under the wrath of God
    C. Awaiting God's judgment
II. The subjective problem within himself
    A. Deadened in his spirit
    B. Ruined in his soul
    C. Corrupted in his body

Text

I. THE OBJECTIVE PROBLEM BEFORE GOD

As a result of the fall, man's first problem is before God, and it is objective. Objective means something having to do with us but outside of us. Do you remember the illustration of the child who disobeyed his mother and took in the poison? His problem of disobedience to his mother was objective, having to do with him but not something inside of him. By disobeying his mother, he was now in trouble with her and would be punished. Because of our fall in Adam, our objective problem before God is very great, and we will soon face God's punishment.

A. Under God's Condemnation

Because of Adam's disobedience, or transgression, we have all come under God's condemnation (Rom. 5:18a). When God created man, he did not create many men, but only one man. All men were included in this one man. So in God's eyes, when Adam sinned, we were included in this one sin, even though we ourselves may never have sinned in the same way. Because of this, when Adam was judged and came under God's condemnation, we were all judged and came under God's condemnation with him.

B. Under the Wrath of God

Because we were condemned by God in Adam, we are all under the wrath of God (John 3:36b). Because of Adam's sin, all men today are under the wrath of God and awaiting His final judgment.

C. Awaiting God's Judgment

Eventually, because of Adam's sin, man will be judged by God and cast into the lake of fire to suffer God's judgment for eternity (Heb. 9:27). The Bible tells us that God prepared the lake of fire not for man but for Satan and his fallen angels who followed him to rebel against God (Matt. 25:41).

But, because man was deceived and followed Satan to rebel against God by disobeying Him, man must now also suffer God's judgment in the lake of fire with Satan (Rev. 20:15).

Outwardly, and before God, this is the terrible condition into which man fell because of Adam's transgression. Rather than enjoying God's life and expressing Him, man has been condemned to die and to suffer Satan's judgment with him.

II. THE SUBJECTIVE PROBLEM WITHIN HIMSELF

Man's second problem resulting from the fall is subjective, that is, within himself. Using our earlier illustration of the disobedient child, this is the problem of the poison that man took into him, not the problem of his disobedience. By taking in the tree of knowledge, man did not merely do something wrong which could be solved by God's forgiveness. He actually took in the very life of Satan. When this satanic life entered into man, his entire being was deadened, ruined and corrupted.

A. Deadened in His Spirit

First, when the satanic life entered into man, his spirit was deadened. He became dead in sins (Eph. 2:1). Because man's spirit was deadened, it lost its function to contact God and to receive Him as life. Today, because man's spirit has been deadened, men have lost their ability to contact God, and so many do not believe in Him.

B. Ruined in His Soul

When the satanic life entered into man, it ruined man's soul for God's purpose. His mind, which God had created to know God, became darkened and blinded, unable to know Him (Eph. 4:17-18a). His mind became filled with vain thoughts and foolish reasonings that have turned him away from God and His purpose. His emotion, which was created to love God, was turned away from loving Him. Now, man's emotion loves anything and everything else but God and even hates Him (2 Tim. 3:2-4). Finally, his will, which God created for man to choose Him and obey Him, became rebellious against God (Eph. 2:2b). Now man's will has forsaken God and is one with the will of God's enemy, Satan. Because of this, man himself has become the enemy of God.

C. Corrupted in His Body

When Adam took the fruit of the tree of knowledge into him, the sinful life of Satan entered into his body and changed it into the sinful flesh. Now, the sinful life of Satan is in man's body (Rom. 7:17-18a). It is this life, full of lusts and every evil thing, that makes man's body a body of sin, so strong to sin, and a body of death, so weak to serve the Lord and to please Him (Rom. 6:6b; 7:24).

We can see from this that man was condemned by God outwardly, or objectively, and ruined by the satanic life inwardly, or subjectively. Because this sinful life has entered into man, he has even become a child of the Devil (John 8:44; Eph. 2:2b). In such a pitiful and ruined condition, man is helpless to save himself and utterly hopeless. All that he has to look forward to is a life full of sin and God's eternal punishment in the future. This is the condition that all men, including you and I, fell into as the result of Adam's sin. It was such a horrible condition that caused God, in His love, to come to save us.

Questions

1. Define the words "objective" and "subjective."

2. What caused man's objective problem before God?

3. What is man's objective problem before God?

4. What is the cause of man's subjective problem within himself?

5. How has man's three-part being been ruined by the fall?

Further Reference

See Compendium of God's Full Salvation (LSM), Chapter 3.

or

1. The Divine Dispensing of the Divine Trinity (Lee/LSM), p. 17.

2. The Completing Ministry of Paul (Lee/LSM), pp. 57-60.

3. Life-study of Exodus (Lee/LSM), pp. 796-797.

4. Life-study of Galatians (Lee/LSM), p. 98.

5. Life-study of Romans (Lee/LSM), pp. 34-35, 127-128.

6. Life-study of Genesis (Lee/LSM), p. 241.

7. The Kingdom (Lee/LSM), pp. 66-67, 210-211.

8. Life-study of John (Lee/LSM), p. 115.

9. Life-study of Revelation (Lee/LSM), pp. 23, 560-561, 665-668.

THE SOURCE OF SALVATION—GOD'S LOVE

Scripture Reading

Eph. 2:4-5; Titus 3:4-7; John 3:16; 1 John 3:11; 4:9-10;
Rom. 5:8; 1 John 3:1; 1 Pet. 1:3; John 17:23;
2 Thes. 2:16-17; 2 Cor. 5:14-15; Gal. 2:20

Outline

I. Man's hopeless condition
II. God's love for man
III. Mercy reaching further than love
IV. God's love—the source of salvation
V. God's love is eternal

I. MAN'S HOPELESS CONDITION

We have now seen a general picture of man's fallen condition. He has sinned by disobeying God's commandment and come under God's condemnation. He also now has within him the sinful life of God's enemy, Satan. Man is helpless, unable to save himself or others from God's coming judgment. He is also unable to keep himself from sinning and offending God still more. His final destination is the lake of fire, which has been prepared by God for Satan and all those who have followed him. So, in every way, man is both helpless and hopeless.

II. GOD'S LOVE FOR MAN

Yes, man is hopeless in himself. But God loves man because His heart is a heart of love. He loved man in His purpose before He created the heavens and the earth. He loved man after He created him and put him in front of the tree of life. And now, after the fall, He still loves man. God still wants man to be filled up with Him so that man may fully satisfy God's heart by expressing Him.

Let us read Ephesians 2:4-5: "But God, being rich in mercy because of His great love with which He loved us, even when we were dead in offenses, made us alive together with Christ (by grace you have been saved)."

[Verse 4, which tells us that God is rich in mercy, begins with the words "But God." This was the turning factor in our position. We were in a miserable situation, but God came in with His rich mercy to make us suitable for His love.]

iii. Mercy Reaching Further
Than Love

[God is rich in mercy "because of His great love with which He loved us" (v. 4). The object of love should be in a condition deserving love, but the object of mercy is always in a pitiful situation. Hence, God's mercy reaches further than His love. God loves us because we are the object of His selection. But we became pitiful by our fall, even dead in our offenses and sins; therefore, we need God's mercy. Because of His great love, God is rich in mercy to save us from our wretched position to a condition which is suitable for His love.]

iv. God's Love—
The Source of Salvation

This love is the source of our salvation. He manifested this love by sending His only begotten Son to die for our redemption. He did not need to save us. He could have cast us into the lake of fire, but His love caused Him to come and die for us. What a wonderful love!

[The Good Shepherd forsook all to seek one lost sheep. He did not come to seek to save the lost sheep because there were ninety-nine of them. The Good Shepherd came for one lost sheep. In other words, even if only one person in the whole world were lost, the Lord would still have come to the earth. Of course, historically, all men needed to be saved. But as far as the love in His heart is concerned, He was ready to come for one man, for one lost sheep. The Holy Spirit did not begin searching because ten coins were lost; He searched because one coin was lost. The Father did not wait for His prodigal because all of His sons had become prodigal; He opened His arms to one prodigal who returned. In the parable in Luke 15, we see that in the work of His redemption, the Lord was willing to spend Himself freely to meet the need of even one soul....This shows the intense love that the Lord has for man.

The Lord Jesus came to the earth for man. According to Mark 10, He came to serve men even to the point of giving His life as a ransom....He was interested in man, and He considered man precious and worthy of love and service. He served man to such an extent that He met their need by becoming their Savior. This is why He gave His life as a ransom.]

V. GOD'S LOVE IS ETERNAL

Because of this love, we can become children of God to grow to become His sons. First John 3:1 says, "See what manner of love the Father has given to us, that we should be called children of God; and we are. Because of this the world does not know us, because it did not know Him."

Now you can see that because God loves us, we are not a hopeless race of people. He wants to save us and to give us His life. His purpose with man is eternal, and so is His love. He never changes. When He loves us, He loves us eternally. Even when we fell into sin and death, His mercy reached us. Hallelujah! Because of His great love for us, it is guaranteed that we will be filled with His life and fulfill His eternal purpose.

Questions

1. Why does God love man?

2. With what kind of love has God loved man?

3. How did God show His love for man?

4. What has God's love accomplished for us according to Eph. 2:4-5 and 1 John 3:1?

5. Since God loved us and accomplished so much for us, what should our response be to such a love?

Quoted Portions

1. Life-study of Ephesians (Lee/LSM), p. 179.

2. The Character of the Lord's Worker (Nee/LSM), pp. 21, 19.

Further Reference

See Compendium of God's Full Salvation (LSM), Chapter 6.

or

1. Life-study of Romans (Lee/LSM), pp. 102-103, 255-257, 374-375.

2. Life-study of Ephesians (Lee/LSM), p. 179.

3. Life-study of Titus (Lee/LSM), pp. 40-41.

4. The Character of the Lord's Worker (Nee/LSM), pp. 16-21.

5. Gospel Outlines (Lee/LSM), pp. 330-331.

6. Life-study of Second Thessalonians (Lee/LSM), p. 34.

7. Life-study of Second Corinthians (Lee/LSM), p. 120.

8. Life-study of Hebrews (Lee/LSM), p. 230.

9. Twelve Baskets Full Vol. 1 (Nee/LSM), p. 54.

10. Life-study of John (Lee/LSM), p. 490.

Lesson Nine

THE BASIS OF SALVATION—
GOD'S RIGHTEOUSNESS

Scripture Reading

Rom. 3:21-22; 1:17; 10:3;
Phil. 3:9; 2 Pet. 1:1; Rom. 8:3

Outline

I. The righteousness of God is God Himself
II. Man under condemnation because of God's righteousness
III. Christ died to fulfill God's righteous requirement
IV. God's love, righteousness, and wisdom

Text

In this lesson, we are covering the matter of God's righteousness. It is the basis upon which we can be saved. Don't be frightened by the term "righteousness." If you know what it is, you will rejoice and praise Him. Without the righteousness of God, we would not be so bold to come to God to accept and enjoy His salvation.

I. THE RIGHTEOUSNESS OF GOD
IS GOD HIMSELF

First, let us see what the righteousness of God is. [We may say that the righteousness of God is what God is with respect to justice and rightness (Rom. 3:21-22; 1:17; 10:3; Phil. 3:9). God is just and right. Whatever God is in His justice and rightness constitutes His righteousness. Furthermore, all that God is in His justice and rightness is actually Himself. Therefore, the righteousness of God is God Himself. The righteousness of God is a Person, not merely a divine attribute.]

II. MAN UNDER CONDEMNATION BECAUSE
OF GOD'S RIGHTEOUSNESS

God has a big problem on His hands because of our sin. Remember, He said in Genesis 2:17 that if the man whom He loved ate of the tree of knowledge, he would surely die. Man ate of that cursed tree, so according to God's righteousness we must die. Righteousness and justice are the foundation of God's throne. If God did not condemn man, Satan could come in to rightfully accuse God of being unrighteous. If this happened, God would have no authority to rule and the whole universe would be turned upside down.

III. CHRIST DIED TO FULFILL
GOD'S RIGHTEOUS REQUIREMENT

God loves man, yet He had to condemn him because of what man had done. Now, what can God do so that He can fulfill His righteousness and yet keep the man whom He has loved? How can He forgive the man He loves without violating His righteousness? The answer is God's twofold righteousness.

[In order that God might be able to forgive us, Christ, the Son of God, became flesh. As (Romans) 8:3 says, God sent His own Son in the likeness of the flesh of sin. By incarnation, the Lord took upon Himself the likeness of the flesh of sin and became identified with sinners in the flesh. For the sake of God's righteousness, the Lord Jesus was put to death on the cross. There, on the cross, He was made sin for us, and God condemned sin in the flesh. By dying on our behalf the Lord accomplished redemption and fulfilled all of God's righteous requirements. Now God has the position righteously to forgive us. In fact, He not only can forgive us, but, for the sake of His righteousness, He must forgive us. God forgives not primarily because He loves us, but because He is bound by His righteousness to do so.]

IV. GOD'S LOVE, RIGHTEOUSNESS, AND WISDOM

God's righteousness condemns us, but by Christ's righteous death we are justified. Christ's righteous death fulfills

God's righteous requirements. How wonderful this is! Man is forgiven—saved. At the same time, God's righteousness is maintained and Satan's mouth is shut. Now, God cannot condemn those who believe in Christ's righteous death and neither can Satan. By seeing this, we will love and appreciate our God. Through His twofold righteousness, we can see His love, His righteousness, and His wisdom.

Questions

1. What is God's righteousness?

2. Why did man have to die for his sins even though God loved him?

3. What steps did God take to satisfy His righteousness while at the same time saving man for His purpose?

4. How did Christ's death fulfill God's righteousness?

5. When God forgives and saves us is it based on His love for man or on His righteousness? Why?

Quoted Portions

1. Life-study of Romans (Lee/LSM), pp. 49, 598.

Further Reference

See Compendium of God's Full Salvation (LSM), Chapter 7.

or

1. Life-study of Romans (Lee/LSM), pp. 49, 597-600, 602-607, 636, 638-639.

2. Life-study of Second Corinthians (Lee/LSM), pp. 132, 246.

3. Life-study of Second Peter (Lee/LSM), pp. 5-6, 113-114.

4. Life-study of Hebrews (Lee/LSM), pp. 161-162.

5. The New Covenant (Nee/LSM), p. 58.

Lesson Ten

THE SAVIOR-GOD

Scripture Reading

Gen. 3:15; 22:18; Isa. 7:14; 9:6; John 1:1, 14; 1 Pet. 3:18;
John 1:29; 3:14; 12:24; 1 Cor. 15:45b; Gal. 3:14

Outline

   I. Man's birthright—to contain God as life
  II. The Savior promised by God.
 III. The Savior prophesied by God
 IV. The God-man Savior
     A. Incarnated
     B. Crucified
     C. Resurrected

Text

God is not only our Judge because of His righteousness,
but He is also our Savior-God because He loves us. God
judged man according to His righteousness after man sinned
in the garden of Eden; yet because He loved man, He also
promised to save him.

I. MAN'S BIRTHRIGHT—
TO CONTAIN GOD AS LIFE

Man was made by God to contain Him as life. This is man's
birthright. A birthright means something that is rightfully
yours by birth. The birthright of a young prince is the king-
ship, that is, to become the king to rule and to enjoy all the
privileges of being king. If the prince were kidnapped
and taken away to another land, he would lose his birthright, even though he is still the son of the king. When man
was deceived by Satan to disobey God and to take in the
satanic life and nature, he was kidnapped away from God's
purpose and lost his birthright to contain God as life. Man is

"kidnapped" and under the control of Satan. Because of this, he has lost God as life.

II. THE SAVIOR PROMISED BY GOD

To take care of both problems, God gave man two main promises. God promised to rescue man from Satan's control. He also promised to give His life to man to fulfill His purpose.

In Genesis 3:15, God promised that the seed of woman would come to bruise the head of the serpent. In Genesis 22:18, God promised that in the seed of Abraham all the nations would be blessed.

III. THE SAVIOR PROPHESIED BY GOD

According to these promises God prophesied in the Old Testament concerning this coming One who is just God Himself coming in the flesh to save man.

First, the Old Testament prophesies concerning His birth; that is, of whom He would be born (Isa. 7:14) and where (Micah 5:2). Next, it tells us how He would look (Isa. 52:14; 53:2) and how He would minister (Isa. 61:1; 42:1). Then, it foretells the year, the month, the day, the place and the way in which He would die (Dan. 9:24-26; Exo. 12:1-6; Gen. 22:2; Deut. 21:23; Zech. 12:10; Psa. 34:20). It tells in a picture that He would enter into death and the tomb and resurrect on the third day to become a sign to that generation for repentance (Jonah 1:2, 17; 3:2-10; Matt. 12:40). When Christ came, He fulfilled all these promises and prophecies. How marvelous! The subject of the entire Old Testament is just this wonderful One, this One promised and prophesied by God.

IV. THE GOD-MAN SAVIOR

A. Incarnated

John 1:1 says that the Word was God. John 1:14 says that the Word became flesh. This Word who became flesh is Jesus Christ. He is truly God and truly man. When He came, He fulfilled all of the promises and prophecies of God in the Old Testament. As the God-man, He was born of a virgin in Bethlehem, and lived for thirty-three and a half years as a genuine human being, yet without sin. Then He was crucified in the year, month, day and place which were prophesied hundreds of years earlier.

B. Crucified

The death of Christ has accomplished many wonderful things for us. We are redeemed, forgiven, washed, justified and reconciled to God. Redeemed means a price has been paid to buy us back to God. Justified means God considers us to be as righteous as He is. Reconciled means that we, who were God's enemies, have now made up with God. On top of all that, His death also bruised Satan's head, as God had promised to do in Genesis 3:15. (See Heb. 2:14.)

C. Resurrected

On the third day, He resurrected to become the life-giving Spirit to give life to man, thus fulfilling the promise in Genesis 22:18. (See Gal. 3:14.) He became the promised Spirit to give man life as the eternal blessing. How wonderful! Man's negative problem was solved and his birthright was restored by the death of this Man, Jesus Christ. All of man's problems with sins before God were solved, and the head of Satan, the serpent who had kidnapped man, was crushed. Now, man can believe in this Jesus to be saved from sin and death, and to receive the life of God to fulfill God's eternal purpose. We have been restored back to God and can now enjoy our birthright, which is to contain God's life. We need to praise and love our Savior-God for all that He has done.

Questions

1. What does the word "birthright" mean? What is man's birthright? Why does man have such a birthright?

2. What are the two main promises of God in the Old Testament? How do they relate to man's problems?

3. Read the verses on the prophecies concerning Christ given in the lesson and list what they tell you of Christ before He came.

4. What do we mean when we say that Christ was a God-man?

5. What was accomplished by Christ's death and resurrection?

6. How are these accomplishments applied to us for our salvation?

Further Reference

See Compendium of God's Full Salvation (LSM),
Chapter 8 and 9.

or

1. The Divine Dispensing of the Divine Trinity (Lee/LSM), pp. 17-18.

2. Life-study of Genesis (Lee/LSM), pp. 266, 767-768.

3. The Kernel of the Bible (Lee/LSM), pp. 124, 136.

4. Life-study of Galatians (Lee/LSM), pp. 107, 130-131, 172-173.

5. Life-study of Matthew (Lee/LSM), pp. 43, 59, 61-62, 84, 130, 151-153, 212, 418-419, 565-566, 660-663, 791, 811-812, 823.

6. Life-study of First Peter (Lee/LSM), pp. 72-75, 98, 105.

7. Life-study of Second Thessalonians (Lee/LSM), pp. 22-23.

8. Life-study of Exodus (Lee/LSM), pp. 164, 202-203, 248-252, 857, 1117, 1178, 1229, 1237, 1729.

9. Life-study of John (Lee/LSM), pp. 21-22, 29, 32-33, 37, 112-113, 315-318, 437-438, 521-522.

10. Christ and the Church in Psalms (Lee/LSM), pp. 35, 46.

11. The Mending Ministry of John (Lee/LSM), pp. 3-6.

12. The Stream (Lee/LSM), vol. 6, no. 2, pp. 2-3.

13. Experiencing Christ as the Offerings for the Church Meetings (Lee/LSM), p. 71.

14. Life-study of Hebrews (Lee/LSM), pp. 9, 38, 50, 91-93, 102-104, 124, 135, 137, 141, 145-147, 312-313.

15. Life-study of Colossians (Lee/LSM), pp. 66-67, 77-81, 190-191.

16. The Kingdom (Lee/LSM), p. 41.

17. Life-study of Romans (Lee/LSM), pp. 21-22, 145, 186, 398, 567-568, 627, 639.

18. Life-study of Philippians (Lee/LSM), pp. 86-88.

19. The Four Major Steps of Christ (Lee/LSM), pp. 8-15.

20. The Stream (Lee/LSM), vol. 3, no. 2, p. 5; vol. 10, no. 1, p. 18; vol. 13, no. 4, p. 9.

21. Life-study of First Corinthians (Lee/LSM), pp. 71-72, 598, 613-614.

22. The Glorious Church (Nee/LSM), pp. 18-19.

23. Life-study of Ephesians (Lee/LSM), pp. 57-58, 205-206, 226, 723, 728-729.

24. Life-study of Second Corinthians (Lee/LSM), pp. 129-130, 328.

25. The Economy of God (Lee/LSM), p. 127.

26. Life-study of First John (Lee/LSM), pp. 69-70.

27. Life-study of Revelation (Lee/LSM), pp. 44, 740-741.

28. The Spirit and Body (Lee/LSM), pp. 83-85.

29. The Kernel of the Bible (Lee/LSM), pp. 124, 136.

30. The Experience of Life (Lee/LSM), p. 29.

Lesson Eleven

REDEMPTION

Scripture Reading

Eph. 1:7; Gal. 3:13; 1 Pet. 2:24; 3:18; 2 Cor. 5:21;
Heb. 10:12; 9:28, 12, 14; 1 Pet. 1:18-19

Outline

I. What is redemption?—to repossess at a cost
II. Lost because of sin
III. Redeemed by Christ's blood

Text

In this lesson, we begin to cover five objective aspects of God's full salvation that solved our problem before God. The first item is the redemption which Christ accomplished for us by His death on the cross. First, read Ephesians 1:7: "In whom we have redemption through His blood, the forgiveness of offenses, according to the riches of His grace."

I. WHAT IS REDEMPTION?— TO REPOSSESS AT A COST

What is redemption? Redemption is the noun form of the word "redeem." [The word redeem means to purchase back something which originally was yours but which had become lost. This hymnal belongs to me. If the hymnal becomes lost and I pay the price of buying it back, I would be redeeming the hymnal. Thus, redemption means to repossess at a cost.

We originally belonged to God. We were His possession. However, we were lost. Nevertheless, God did not give us up. He paid the price to have us back, repossessing us at a great cost. This is redemption. Even after we had become lost, He desired to regain us. However, this was not easy for God to do because our being lost involved us in sins and in many other things that were against His righteousness, holiness, and glory. Because we were lost, we had many problems with God in respect to His righteousness, holiness, and glory. We were under a threefold demand, the demand of righteousness, holiness, and glory. Many requirements were laid upon us, and it was impossible for us to fulfill them. The price was too great. God paid the price for us, repossessing us at a tremendous cost. Christ died on the cross to accomplish eternal redemption for us (Gal. 3:13; 1 Pet. 2:24; 3:18; 2 Cor. 5:21; Heb. 10:12; 9:28). His blood has obtained eternal redemption for us (Heb. 9:12, 14; 1 Pet. 1:18-19).]

II. LOST BECAUSE OF SIN

We are not righteous according to God's righteousness. We are not holy as God is holy. Our destiny was holiness, but we fell from it and received a sinful nature. As a result, we are not expressing God, but expressing Satan. So, we have come very short of God's glory. What a dreadful condition!

Because of sin, transgression, and lawlessness, we became lost. We were under the demand of the law, and, according to this law, we were cursed to die.

III. REDEEMED BY CHRIST'S BLOOD

But, praise the Lord! Jesus Christ came to redeem us. By His righteous death, He redeemed us back to God and to His purpose. To accomplish this, His precious blood was the price. Because we could not pay such a high price, He paid it for us. We were destined to die in sin, but now we may come back to God, be forgiven by God, receive God's life, be filled with Him, and express Him. What a wonderful redemption!

Questions

1. What is the meaning of the word "redeem"? How does it apply to God and man?

2. What is the price that God paid for us?

Quoted Portions

1. Life-study of Romans (Lee/LSM), pp. 55-56.

Further Reference

See Compendium of God's Full Salvation (LSM), Chapter 11.

or

1. Life-study of Romans (Lee/LSM), pp. 55-56.

2. Life-study of Titus (Lee/LSM), pp. 35-36.

3. Life-study of Exodus (Lee/LSM), p. 1541.

4. Life-study of First John (Lee/LSM), pp. 54-55.

5. Life-study of Galatians (Lee/LSM), pp. 106-107, 166, 191.

6. Life-study of First Peter (Lee/LSM), pp. 97-98, 103-104, 216-217.

7. Life-study of Ephesians (Lee/LSM), pp. 195-196.

Lesson Twelve

FORGIVENESS AND CLEANSING OF SINS

Scripture Reading

Jer. 31:34; Zech. 13:1; Matt. 26:28;
Heb. 9:12-14, 22-23; 1 John 1:7-9; Rev. 1:5

Outline

I. Forgiveness of Sins
   A. Forgetting our Sins
   B. Forgiveness
II. Cleansing

Text

I. FORGIVENESS OF SINS

After sinning against God, man needed God's forgiveness
and cleansing of sins. Since we have offended God, we need
His forgiveness; yet we cannot be forgiven before His righteousness is fulfilled. So, we must die to satisfy God's
righteousness. But, if we die, God would have no one to
receive His life for the fulfillment of His eternal purpose. The
perfect solution to this problem was for Christ to come and
die for us. Because of His death, God's righteous requirement
has been met, and we can now be forgiven by God.

A. Forgetting Our Sins

According to Jeremiah 31:34, for God to forgive our sins is
for Him to forget them, too. When we forgive someone for
offending us, we seldom forget what they did to us. However,
God is different. When He forgives our sins, He does not
remember them anymore. Hallelujah! Because of Christ's
death and our believing in Him, we can be forgiven by God.
When God forgives our sins, He forgets them. To Him, it is
just as though we have never sinned! Just by believing this,
you are forgiven!

B. Forgiveness

[The Son's redemption through His blood is the forgiveness of our offenses (Matt. 26:28; Heb. 9:22). Redemption is what Christ has accomplished for our offenses; forgiveness is what Christ accomplished applied to our offenses. Redemption was accomplished on the cross, whereas forgiveness is applied the moment we believe in Christ. Redemption and forgiveness are actually two ends of one thing. We have seen that the forgiveness of offenses is the redemption accomplished through the blood of Christ. However, two terms are used because this one thing has two ends: the end of the accomplishment on the cross and the end of the application to us at the time we believed. Although redemption was accomplished on the cross when Christ shed His blood, it was not applied to us at that time. The application did not take place until we believed in Christ and made confession to the righteous God. At that very moment, the Spirit of God applied to us the redemption Christ had accomplished on the cross. Hence, redemption is the accomplishment, and forgiveness is the application.]

II. CLEANSING

[What is the difference between forgiving and cleansing? In order to know this difference, we need to know the difference between sins and unrighteousness. Sins refer to offenses, and unrighteousness is the mark, the stain, on our behavior caused by the committing of an offense. Whenever we sin, we commit an offense. This offense then becomes a stain on our behavior, and this stain is unrighteousness. For instance, suppose you buy two items, but you are charged only for one. If you pay for just one item, that will be an act of sinning against the store. With respect to the person who sold you the items, that is an offense. But with respect to your character, that is a mark of unrighteousness. For this reason, others would not say that you are sinful, but would say that you are unrighteous.

In a similar way, when we commit sins before God, with respect to God those sins are offenses. But with respect to us, they are stains of unrighteousness. We need to confess our sins. Then, on the one hand, God forgives our sins, our offenses. On the other hand, God washes away the mark, the stain, of our unrighteousness. This is the reason John in (1 John) 1:9 speaks both of the forgiveness of sins and the cleansing from unrighteousness. The forgiveness of sins is actually the cleansing, the washing away, of the stain of our unrighteousness.]

Questions

1. Why does man need God's forgiveness and cleansing?

2. How is God able to forgive man righteously?

3. How does God's way of forgiving differ from our way?

4. What is the difference between forgiveness and cleansing?

5. What is the distinction between redemption and forgiveness?

6. Have you experienced God's forgiveness of your sins?

Quoted Portions

1. Life-study of Ephesians (Lee/LSM), pp. 57-58.

2. Life-study of First John (Lee/LSM), pp. 104-105.

Further Reference

See Compendium of God's Full Salvation (LSM), Chapter 12 and 13.

or

1. Life-study of Hebrews (Lee/LSM), p. 144.

2. Life-study of Matthew (Lee/LSM), p. 604.

3. Life-study of Ephesians (Lee/LSM), pp. 57-58, 60-61.

4. Life-study of Exodus (Lee/LSM), p. 924.

5. Life-study of Romans (Lee/LSM), p. 598.

6. Life-study of John (Lee/LSM), pp. 104-105.

7. Life-study of Hebrews (Lee/LSM), pp. 9, 38.

8. Life-study of First John (Lee/LSM), pp. 67-69.

Lesson Thirteen

JUSTIFICATION

Scripture Reading

Rom. 3:22-24, 28; 4:25; 5:1; 8:33-34

Outline

I. Justification by faith
II. Based upon Christ's redemption

Text

Romans chapter three, verses 23-26 says, "For all have sinned and come short of the glory of God; being justified freely by His grace through the redemption in Christ Jesus: whom God set forth a propitiation-cover through faith in His blood, for the showing forth of His righteousness in respect of the passing by of the sins that occurred before in the forbearance of God; for the showing forth of His righteousness in the present time, that He should be just and justify the one who is of the faith of Jesus."

I. JUSTIFICATION BY FAITH

[What is justification? Justification is God's action in approving people according to His standard of righteousness. His righteousness is the standard, not ours. Although we think we are righteous, our righteousness is only a quarter inch high. Regardless of how righteous we are or how righteous we think we are, our righteousness is just a fraction of an inch high. How high is God's righteousness? It is unlimited! Can you be approved by God according to your own righteousness? This is impossible. Although you may be right with everyone—with your parents, your children, and your friends—your righteousness will never justify you before God. You may justify yourself according to your standard of righteousness, but that does not enable you to be

justified by God according to His standard. We need justification by faith. Justification by faith before God means we are
approved by God according to the standard of His righteousness.

How can God do this? He can do it because our justification is based upon the redemption of Christ. When the
redemption of Christ is applied to us, we are justified. If there
were no such redemption, it would be impossible for us to be
justified by God. Redemption is the basis of justification.]

Are you justified? How were you justified? The Bible tells
us that we were justified by faith in Christ, not by works
(Rom. 3:28, 5:1).

II. BASED UPON CHRIST'S REDEMPTION

Christ's death accomplished redemption for us. Based
upon His redemptive death, God justified us. "Who shall
bring a charge against God's chosen ones? It is God who
justifies. Who is he that condemns? It is Christ Jesus
who died, but rather who was raised..." (Rom. 8:33-34).
Because Christ has died already, whoever is of the faith of
Jesus is justified.

God is righteous. He cannot allow Christ to die for nothing. Since Christ died for us, then we are all justified. God
cannot make His claim on Christ and then again on us. Since
Christ paid the price, there is no need for us to pay it again.
We are justified simply by believing in Him. Praise the Lord!

Because of God's righteousness, we were condemned.
Because of Christ's one righteous act, His death on the cross
for our sins, we are all justified according to God's righteousness. Now we can say to God, "By believing in Christ, I
am as righteous as You." Would you dare to say this? If
you believe the Bible, repent for your sins and believe in
Christ, you would certainly say this. This is the basic
Christian faith.

Questions

1. What is the basic meaning of being justified by faith?

2. What is the main thing we should be impressed with concerning justification?

3. How can God approve us according to His righteous standard?

4. What is your condition before God now that you have been justified?

Quoted Portions

1. Life-study of Romans (Lee/LSM), p. 51.

Further Reference

See Compendium of God's Full Salvation (LSM), Chapter 14.

or

1. Life-study of Romans (Lee/LSM), pp. 11, 51, 60-61, 77, 82-83, 460-461.

2. Life-study of Second Corinthians (Lee/LSM), pp. 165-166.

3. Life-study of Genesis (Lee/LSM), p. 604.

Lesson Fourteen

RECONCILIATION

Scripture Reading

Rom. 5:1, 10-11; Col. 1:20-22; 2 Cor. 5:18-19; Eph. 2:13-18

Outline

I. Man—God's enemy
II. Reconciled by Christ's death

Text

Now, we come to the last objective point of God's full salvation—reconciliation. Reconciliation means the action of bringing two parties back into oneness or harmony.

The Apostle Paul said, "Therefore, having been justified by faith, we have peace toward God through our Lord Jesus Christ" (Rom. 5:1). He also said, "For if, while we were enemies, we were reconciled to God through the death of His Son, much more, having been reconciled, we shall be saved in His life. And not only so, but we also are boasting in God through our Lord Jesus Christ, through whom we have now received the reconciliation" (Rom. 5:10-11).

I. MAN—GOD'S ENEMY

[Originally, we were not only sinners, but also enemies of God. Through the redeeming death of Christ, God has justified us, the sinners, and has reconciled us, His enemies to Himself (5:1, 10-11). This transpired when we believed in the Lord Jesus. We have received God's justification and reconciliation by faith. This has opened the way and ushered us into the realm of grace for the enjoyment of God.]

At the fall, man not only sinned against God, but also became the enemy of God. For sins, forgiveness is enough; but because man has become God's enemy, he needs something more. He needs to be reconciled.

If you become someone's enemy, you need to be reconciled to him. Without reconciliation, you would probably never talk to him. If you see him, you may avoid him. When you are in class, you would not look at him. But, if another friend would reconcile you to him, then you can make up and be his friend again.

God loves man and wants to be his life. Man may fulfill God's eternal purpose by being filled with God. But now, since we have become God's enemies, His purpose cannot be fulfilled with us. Reconciliation is necessary for us to bring us back to God. We praise the Lord that He came in the Son to die for us.

II. RECONCILED BY CHRIST'S DEATH

Christ's death solved the problem of our offending God's righteousness. Therefore, it is by His death that we are reconciled to God (Rom. 5:10a). Man has been reconciled to God, so man and God can now be in harmony. Hallelujah for His redeeming death! It took care of all our objective problems. Christ paid the price for our sins to redeem us back. When we believe in Him, His redemption is applied to us and we are forgiven and cleansed from our sins. Now God considers us to be as righteous as He is. Hallelujah! Satan still has a problem with God, but we don't. Now we can freely come to God to receive Him as our life. Praise the Lord! God is happy. His angels are happy. His church is happy!

Questions

1. Define "reconciliation."

2. Why does man need to be reconciled to God?

3. Why is man an enemy of God?

4. How did Christ's death reconcile us to God?

5. Now that we have been reconciled to God what is our relationship with Him?

6. Are there any problems now that remain unsolved between you and God? Explain your answer.

Quoted Portions

1. Life-study of Romans (Lee/LSM), p. 102.

Further Reference

See Compendium of God's Full Salvation (LSM),
Chapter 15.

or

1. Life-study of Romans (Lee/LSM), pp. 54-56, 102.

2. Life-study of Ephesians (Lee/LSM), pp. 197, 226-228, 599.

3. Life-study of Second Corinthians (Lee/LSM), p. 132.

Lesson Fifteen

REGENERATION

Scripture Reading

John 3:2-6; 1:12-13; 1 John 5:12;
Ezek. 36:26-27

Outline

I. God's intention
II. The need of God's life
III. Born of God
IV. A new heart, a new spirit, and the indwelling Spirit

Text

With this lesson, we come to the first of five subjective aspects of God's full salvation—regeneration. Regeneration means that in addition to the life we received at our birth, we receive another life, the life of God. This is what the Bible means when it speaks of being "born again" or "born anew." Regeneration is the center of our salvation experience. It is the beginning point of our life relationship with God.

I. GOD'S INTENTION

God's intention is to have a group of people filled with Himself as their life that they may express Him in His image and represent Him with His authority. Adam's disobedience caused him to fall into sin and to lose this birthright. Christ's death took care of all of man's problems before God. It enabled God to redeem, forgive, cleanse and justify man according to His own righteousness, not simply because He loved man. Now we have been brought back fully to God. Until man contains God as life in order to express Him, neither God nor man can be satisfied.

The next step God takes in His full salvation is to enter into man to put His life into him. This is the most crucial step. Even if man were completely forgiven and reconciled, he still could not express God without receiving His life.

II. THE NEED OF GOD'S LIFE

In John 3, Jesus spoke to a good man named Nicodemus. He was a very wise and moral man, but the Lord Jesus told him that he needed to be born of water and of the Spirit. In his behavior and living Nicodemus was a moral man, but in God's eyes, he had the satanic life and nature. Because of this, he needed to be born of water. Jesus was speaking of the water of baptism. In the Bible, baptism means termination. Termination ends our sinful and natural life. The satanic life and nature which Nicodemus had received from the fall in Adam had to be terminated. Then, the life of God, which has come from the life-giving Spirit in Christ's resurrection, could be germinated in him.

III. BORN OF GOD

To be a Christian is not a matter of being improved. To be a Christian is to be born of God, which means that in addition to our human life, we receive God's life. Because we were all born in sin, we are all sinners. How can a sinner stop sinning? It is not possible. How can you tell a dog to stop barking and to start meowing? What you do is governed by your life. Even though you are forgiven by God for your sins, your sinful nature will cause you to sin again. What you need is another life, a sinless life. The only life that is without sin is God's life. Regeneration brings this life into you. This is the life that Adam gave up when he turned from the tree of life to the tree of knowledge. Now, by believing into Christ, we can be born of God and receive Him as life. Praise the Lord!

After receiving God's life, the satanic nature within man is annulled. Sinful, lowly men like us can now grow in God's life to become the sons of God to express Him.

IV. A NEW HEART, A NEW SPIRIT, AND THE INDWELLING SPIRIT

Ezekiel 36:26-27 tells us that at regeneration, we receive three wonderful things. First, we receive a "new heart," a "heart of flesh," to replace our old "stony heart." By experiencing the love of God in grace, our old heart, which formerly was cold and hard toward the Lord, is softened to love and desire Him. Second, we receive a "new spirit." This is our old, deadened spirit renewed and enlivened by the life-giving Spirit. Now, our spirit is alive and can fully function to contact God's Spirit and to enjoy His full salvation. Third, we receive the Spirit of God Himself to come to indwell us. What a wonderful salvation we receive through believing in the Lord! Regeneration is the center and beginning of this salvation.

Questions

1. What does it mean to be born again?

2. Why do we need regeneration?

3. Why did Jesus tell Nicodemus that besides being born of the Spirit he also needed to be born of water? How does this apply to us?

4. What does regeneration have to do with accomplishing God's purpose?

5. What three things do we receive as a result of our regeneration?

Further Reference

See Compendium of God's Full Salvation (LSM), Chapter 16.

or

1. The Knowledge of Life (Lee/LSM), pp. 25-27, 35-36, 43.

2. Life-study of John (Lee/LSM), pp. 26-27, 95-96, 98, 105, 107-108.

3. Life-study of Galatians (Lee/LSM), pp. 279-280.

4. What is Regeneration? pp. 6-7.

5. The Experience of Life (Lee/LSM), pp. 11-12.

6. The Fulfillment of the Tabernacle and Offerings in the Writings of John (Lee/LSM), pp. 62, 84-88.

7. Life-study of Romans (Lee/LSM), p. 217.

8. The Kingdom (Lee/LSM), pp. 13-14.

Lesson Sixteen

SANCTIFICATION

Scripture Reading

1 Thes. 5:23; Rom. 5:10; 1 Pet. 2:2; Rom. 1:4;
Eph. 5:26; John 17:17; 6:63

Outline

I. To be made holy
II. Holiness is God Himself
III. Growth
IV. By His life
V. Through the Spirit and the Word

Text

Praise the Lord for regeneration. Through it we have received a new life, a new heart, and a new spirit. The Spirit of God is now dwelling within us. Our spirit, which had been deadened by man's fall, has now been made alive by the life-giving Spirit. We have now begun to subjectively experience God's full salvation. Praise Him for this wonderful new beginning!

But is this all there is to God's salvation? Certainly not. Several more things must take place for God's full salvation to be completed. In this lesson we will talk about sanctification. Sanctification is the working of God's holy nature into us.

I. TO BE MADE HOLY

In order for God's holy nature to be worked into us, sanctification is needed. Sanctification means the process by which something is made holy. Some people think that if you try not to sin, then you are holy. Some think that if you stay away from evil things, then you are holy. But, how can we, the unholy people full of the satanic nature, become holy just by doing or not doing certain things? It is impossible!

II. HOLINESS IS GOD HIMSELF

In the whole universe, God is the only holy One. His life and nature are holy. If you don't have God, you cannot be holy. If you have a little God, you have a little holiness. If you have more God, you have more holiness. If you are full of God, you are full of holiness. Holiness is just God Himself.

III. GROWTH

You have been regenerated by believing in Jesus Christ. Are you holy? If you say yes, then how much? Regeneration is a new birth. Peter tells us that young Christians are newborn babes (1 Pet. 2:2). At regeneration, we were born of God and received God's holy life and nature into us. Therefore, we are a little holy. When we grow in the divine life and nature, we become more holy. The growing of life is the adding of God's holy nature into us. This growth process is called sanctification.

IV. BY HIS LIFE

Romans 5:10 says, "For if, while we were enemies, we were reconciled to God through the death of His Son, much more, having been reconciled, we shall be saved in His life." This verse clearly tells us that the saving in life is "much more" than reconciliation. Reconciliation only took care of our outward problem with God. But being saved in His life saves us from our sinful nature into the divine and holy nature of God. This is sanctification. The Apostle Paul used the words "much more" to show the importance of sanctification in life.

V. THROUGH THE SPIRIT AND THE WORD

The way to be sanctified is to touch the Spirit of holiness (Rom. 1:4). The Lord has come into our spirit through regeneration. When we turn to the Lord and pray, we touch the Spirit of holiness. At that moment, the holy nature spreads into our soul to sanctify us. John 17:17 also tells us that we are sanctified in the truth of the Word. So, we also need to touch the Lord through the Word.

In this lesson, we can see that we should not be satisfied with being forgiven or cleansed by God or even with being regenerated. These things are wonderful but we must go on. We must go on until we reach full maturity in the divine life. When we reach this goal, we will be fully sanctified; that is, we will be saturated with the holy life and nature of God, and able to express and represent Him fully.

Questions

1. What does it mean to be sanctified?

2. What two things take place through sanctification?

3. What is the basic factor of our sanctification?

4. What is the goal of our sanctification?

5. How can we experience sanctification practically?

Further Reference

See Compendium of God's Full Salvation (LSM), Chapter 17.

or

1. Life-study of Hebrews (Lee/LSM), pp. 119-122.

2. Life-study of First Peter (Lee/LSM), pp. 19-20, 32-33, 42-43.

3. Life-study of Ephesians (Lee/LSM), pp. 26, 28-29, 30-31, 37-38, 110, 457-458, 472-473.

4. Life-study of Romans (Lee/LSM), pp. 12, 204, 206-210, 213.

5. Truth Messages (Lee/LSM), pp. 40-43, 46.

6. Life-study of John (Lee/LSM), pp. 481-482, 484-485.

Lesson Seventeen

TRANSFORMATION

Scripture Reading

Rom. 12:2; 2 Cor. 3:16-18; Eph. 4:23; Col. 3:10;
1 Pet. 2:2-5; Eph. 5:26-27; Rom. 8:28-29

Outline

I. An inward change
II. A process of metabolism
III. A new element replacing the old
IV. In our mind, emotion, will
V. By the spreading of Christ
VI. By beholding the Lord with an unveiled face

Text

I. AN INWARD CHANGE

Transformation is the result of sanctification and is related to man's soul. Transformation means that a substance changes in nature and form. This is an inward change in nature that causes an outward change in form.

II. A PROCESS OF METABOLISM

[This type of change is a metabolic change. It is not just an outward change, but a change in inward constitution as well as in external form. This change occurs by the process of metabolism. In the process of metabolism an organic element filled with vitamins comes into our being and produces a chemical change in our organic life. This chemical reaction changes the constitution of our being from one form into another. This is transformation.

Suppose that a person has a very pale complexion and that someone else, wishing to change his colorless complexion, applies some coloring to his skin. This, no doubt, produces an outward change, but it is not an organic change, a change in life. How then can a person truly have a colorful face? By daily absorbing into his body healthy food with the necessary organic elements. Because your body is a living organism, when an organic substance enters into it a chemical compound is formed organically by the process of metabolism. Gradually this inward process will change the coloration of your face. This change is not outward; it is a change from within, a change resulting from the process of metabolism.]

III. A NEW ELEMENT REPLACING THE OLD

[In the process of metabolism a new element is supplied to an organism. This new element replaces the old element and causes it to be discharged. Therefore, as the process of metabolism takes place within a living organism, something new is created within it to replace the old element, which is carried away. Metabolism, therefore, includes three matters: first, the supplying of a new element; second, the replacing of the old element with this new element; and third, the discharge or the removal of the old element so that something new may be produced.]

Through the process of sanctification, the new element of God's life is added into our being. This new element replaces our old, sinful and dead being. This is a continuation of God's salvation within us. We need to be in this process from the day we believe.

IV. IN OUR MIND, EMOTION, WILL

[From the moment we are regenerated in our spirit, it is the Lord's desire that this change of life continue by spreading into our soul, that our mind, our emotion, and our will may all be transformed. Our spirit is regenerated and changed, but our mind, emotion, and will are not transformed and still remain the same. We have Christ as life in our spirit, but we do not have Christ in our soul. We need Christ to continually expand from our spirit into our soul until every part of our soul is transformed into His image (2 Cor. 3:18). Then we will think as He thinks, love as He loves, and choose as He chooses. We will have the likeness of the Lord in our practical life, because our soul is thoroughly saturated with His divine elements.]

V. BY THE SPREADING OF CHRIST

[What is the new element that brings about this inward change? It is Christ, the Triune God, the all-inclusive Spirit. At first this element is only in our spirit. He is confined there, with no way to enter our mind, emotion, and will. If we do not allow Him to spread, our spirit becomes a prison to Him. We need the teaching about transformation by the renewing of the mind. The Spirit wants to spread into our soul, thus adding the new divine element to replace the self. When this new element replacing the old is added to our soul, there will be a change in our mind, emotion, and will.]

VI. BY BEHOLDING THE LORD WITH AN UNVEILED FACE

Second Corinthians 3:18 tells us that we may be "transformed" as we behold the Lord with an unveiled face. This means that we open up to pray to the Lord mainly to fellowship with Him, not to ask Him to do something for us. Don't let anything come in to veil and separate you from Him. When you open up to Him, He may say that the way you talked to your mother was wrong. If you would confess your sins to the Lord and say, "Lord, forgive me," He will come into your soul to transform you. By staying open to Him all the time we can speed up the process of transformation. We all need this process. This is the progress of our Christian life.

Questions

1. How is transformation a result of sanctification?

2. Explain the process of metabolism.

3. What are we being transformed into? (2 Cor. 3:18)

4. How can we speed up the process of transformation?

5. What can hinder or slow down the process of transformation?

6. What will happen to your living the more you are transformed?

Quoted Portions

1. Life-study of Romans (Lee/LSM), p. 293.

2. Life-study of Second Corinthians (Lee/LSM), p. 202.

3. The Parts of Man (Lee/LSM), pp. 16-17.

4. The Completing Ministry of Paul (Lee/LSM), p. 62.

Further Reference

See Compendium of God's Full Salvation (LSM),
Chapter 18.

or

1. The Stream (Lee/LSM), vol. 14, no. 1 , p. 25; no. 3, p. 26.

2. Life-study of Romans (Lee/LSM), pp. 293, 301-302, 500-501.

3. Life-study of Second Corinthians (Lee/LSM), pp. 69-71, 202, 207-208.

4. The Spirit and Body (Lee/LSM), pp. 69-70.

5. The Kingdom (Lee/LSM), pp. 130, 157-159, 200.

6. The Parts of Man (Lee/LSM), pp. 16-17.

7. The Completing Ministry of Paul (Lee/LSM), pp. 62-64.

8. Life-study of Hebrews (Lee/LSM), pp. 376-377.

9. Life-study of Colossians (Lee/LSM), pp. 551-553.

10. The Economy of God (Lee/LSM), pp. 25, 83.

11. Lessons on Prayer (Lee/LSM), p. 88.

12. Life-study of First Corinthians (Lee/LSM), pp. 276-278, 281-282.

13. Life-study of First Peter (Lee/LSM), pp. 134-135, 151-152.

14. Life-study of Ephesians (Lee/LSM), pp. 458-460, 465-468.

15. The Vision of God's Building (Lee/LSM), p. 220.

16. The Knowledge of Life (Lee/LSM), p. 21.

17. The Fulfillment of the Tabernacle and Offerings in the Writings of John (Lee/LSM), pp. 35-36.

18. Life-study of Genesis (Lee/LSM), pp. 157, 876-878.

CONFORMATION

Scripture Reading

Rom. 6:3-5; 8:29; Phil. 3:10, 21; 2 Cor. 3:18;
Eph. 4:20-21

Outline

I. Life-shape, life-power, life-essence
II. Being conformed to the image of Christ
III. By the growth of life and environmental dealings
IV. The mold and the dough
V. Being conformed to the body of the Lord's glory

Text

Romans 8:29 says, "Because whom He foreknew, He also predestinated to be conformed to the image of His Son, that He should be the Firstborn among many brothers."

I. LIFE-SHAPE, LIFE-POWER, LIFE-ESSENCE

[Every life has its own form. For example, a dog has one form and a chicken has another. The growth of a certain life brings in the full form of that life. Today we are sons of God, but we do not yet have the full form, the complete shape, of sons of God. Therefore, by growth and transformation we need to be conformed to the image of Christ. Eventually, we shall be completely conformed to His image. Then we shall possess the full life-shape which comes from the life-power with the life-essence. A carnation, a chicken, and a dog all have a different life-form according to their life-essence. A carnation has the form of a carnation because it has the life-essence of a carnation. The carnation essence develops into the carnation form by means of the life-power within the carnation. Praise the Lord that we have the life-essence and the life-power within us! This life-power is shaping us into the image of the Son of God. Through this shaping function of the life-power, we shall be fully conformed to the image of Christ.]

II. BEING CONFORMED
TO THE IMAGE OF CHRIST

We have been predestinated by God to be conformed to the image of Christ. One day, we will be like Him inside and out. First, Christ died to take care of our objective problem before God. Second, He regenerated us with the divine life by the life-giving Spirit. Third, He is sanctifying us with His holy nature. Fourth, He is transforming us from an old person into a new person. We are being changed in life and nature, not just in outward form. Fifth, He is conforming us to His own image. What a salvation!

III. BY THE GROWTH OF LIFE AND
ENVIRONMENTAL DEALINGS

The life He puts into us grows. As it grows, it sanctifies and transforms us. As we are being transformed, we are being conformed inwardly to His image. On the outside, we have sufferings, but inside of us, the Spirit is working. As we pray or call on His name, we touch Him and He conforms us a little bit more to His image.

IV. THE MOLD AND THE DOUGH

[God's firstborn Son is the prototype, and we are the mass production. Christ is the model, mold, and pattern. God has put us all into Him that we may be molded into the image of His firstborn Son. Eventually we all shall be conformed to the mold. Sometimes when the sisters make cakes they put dough into a mold. By being put into the mold the dough assumes the pattern and image of the mold. Furthermore, the dough must also be baked that the cake may bear the pattern of the mold without any change. If the dough could speak, it probably would cry out, "Sister, have mercy on me. Don't apply so much pressure. I can't bear it. Please keep your hands off." However, the sister would reply, "If I keep my hands off, how will you fit into the pattern of the mold? Dear dough, after my molding you must be put into the oven. You may think that pressure is enough suffering for you, but you also need burning. After you have experienced pressure and intense heat you will bear the pattern of the mold permanently." Likewise, Christ, the firstborn Son of God, is the prototype, pattern, and mold, and we are pieces of dough. We all have been put into the mold, and are now being kneaded by the hand of God.]

Christ is the mold and we are the dough. Through the outward situation and the inward working of the Spirit, we get conformed.

V. BEING CONFORMED TO THE BODY OF THE LORD'S GLORY

As this process is accomplished, our body will be conformed to the body of the Lord's glory (Phil. 3:21). That will be the last great step of conformation. At that time, we will be like Him inwardly and outwardly. This will be the fulfillment of God's eternal purpose. We will be a corporate man in His image to express Him and with His full authority to represent Him for eternity.

Questions

1. Explain the terms "life-shape, life-power, and life-essence."

2. How is conformation related to sanctification and transformation?

3. What two factors are at work to conform us to the image of Christ? Can you give your experience?

4. What will we be like when conformation is completed?

Quoted Portions

1. Life-study of Romans (Lee/LSM), pp. 574, 242.

Further Reference

See Compendium of God's Full Salvation (LSM),
Chapter 19.

or

1. Life-study of Philippians (Lee/LSM), pp. 184-186, 214-215, 459-460, 470.

2. Life-study of Romans (Lee/LSM), pp. 242, 250-251, 492-493, 496, 574.

3. Life-study of Ephesians (Lee/LSM), pp. 45, 393-396.

4. Life-study of Hebrews (Lee/LSM), pp. 388-389.

Lesson Nineteen

GLORIFICATION

Scripture Reading

John 1:14; Rom. 3:23; 8:30; Col. 1:27b; 3:4; 2 Thes. 1:10a

Outline

I. Glory—God expressed
II. The blossoming of the seed
III. Christ in us, the hope of glory
IV. At Christ's second coming

Text

Glorification is the last step of our full salvation. When we are glorified, we reach the climax of God's full salvation and enter into its full enjoyment for eternity. This is the time all Christians look forward to very much. This is our glorious hope.

What is glorification? It is the process of bringing something or someone into glory. Then, what is the meaning of the word "glory" according to the Bible?

I. GLORY—GOD EXPRESSED

Romans 3:23 says, "For all have sinned and come short of the glory of God." According to the Bible, "glory" is just God expressed or the expression of God. When God is hidden, there is no glory. When God is seen and expressed, glory is there.

Man was created to contain the life of God and to express Him with such a life. Therefore, we can say that man was created for glory. But this man sinned, losing his right to receive God's life. Because of this, man could not express God. So the Bible says he has come short of the glory of God. Glorification is God's action in bringing us into the expression of God. He does this in a living way.

II. THE BLOSSOMING OF THE SEED

A carnation seed is a small, round ball and without any beauty, yet it has the life potential to blossom. The blossom is the full expression of all that is in that small seed. It is the glory of that seed. After planting, watering, and growing, this seed becomes a plant. After a while, it blossoms. This blossom is just the seed. When the seed is full-grown, you see a flower. The seed becomes the flower, and the flower is just the seed fully grown. If you have the seed, you have the living hope of the flower. If you have no seed, you have no living, practical hope of a flower. So, within the seed is a flowering life, and this life is the hope of the seed's glory.

III. CHRIST IN US, THE HOPE OF GLORY

Colossians 1:27b says, "Christ in you, the hope of glory." When the gospel was preached to you and you believed, Christ came into you as a seed of life. This seed in you is your hope of glory in the future. Our hope of being brought into the full expression of God is in this seed of Christ.

Today, we don't look glorious. The Christ inside of us has not grown so much. But from regeneration through the process of sanctification, transformation and conformation, Christ is added into us and grows within us just as the carnation seed grows in the soil. One day, when Christ becomes fully grown, He will "blossom" in us. What has been hidden within this seed will be fully expressed, and we will be glorified!

IV. AT CHRIST'S SECOND COMING

Colossians 3:4 tells us that "when Christ our life is manifested, then you also shall be manifested with Him in glory." Christ's second coming, when He comes to the earth again, is His manifestation. If we would live by Christ as our life today, we will be manifested with Him in glory when He appears. We will be glorified. This glory comes out from within us; it does not come upon us suddenly from outside. First, this seed is sown into our spirit. Then, it grows into all the parts of our soul; and finally, it fills and saturates even our physical body, making us just like the Lord Jesus Himself. At that time, we will become the many sons of God in full.

How glorious that day will be. But now, we all must grow in life so that we will blossom in life at that day. It is not a miracle, but a result of life growing. Second Thessalonians 1:10a says, "Whenever He comes to be glorified in His saints." This verse tells us that His coming is our glorification. When He comes, we will be glorified in Him and He will be glorified in us! How marvelous! Through God's salvation, we the sinners become the sons of God, full of God's life and glory in order to express Him for eternity!

Questions

1. What does the word "glorification" mean?

2. In the Bible's concept, what is "glory"?

3. What does the Bible mean when it says that the Christ within us is "the hope of glory"? You may use the illustration of the flower to explain.

4. When will we experience glorification?

5. What is needed today for us to be glorified at Christ's coming? What can we do to meet this need?

Further Reference

See Compendium of God's Full Salvation (LSM),
Chapter 20.

or

1. Life-study of Matthew (Lee/LSM), p. 587.

2. The Parts of Man (Lee/LSM), p. 35.

3. Life-study of Romans (Lee/LSM), pp. 13, 252-254, 494-495, 556, 565-566.

4. Life-study of Colossians (Lee/LSM), pp. 525-526.

5. Life-study of Second Corinthians (Lee/LSM), pp. 105-106.

6. The Kingdom (Lee/LSM), p. 390.

7. Life-study of Hebrews (Lee/LSM), pp. 136-137, 480-481.

8. Life-study of John (Lee/LSM), pp. 458, 491.

9. Life-study of Genesis (Lee/LSM), p. 69.

10. Life-study of Ephesians (Lee/LSM), pp. 168, 314-315, 480-481.

RECEIVING AND GROWING IN SALVATION

Scripture Reading

Rom. 10:8b-15a, 17; Mark 16:16; Acts 2:38; 1 John 1:9; John 6:63; 1 Pet. 2:2; Matt. 4:4; 1 Thes. 5:17; Heb. 10:25.

Outline

I. The initial stage
 A. Hearing the preaching
 B. Repenting
 C. Believing
 D. Confessing
 E. Being baptized
 F. The result
II. The progressing stage
 A. Confessing our sins
 B. Reading His Word
 C. Calling on His name
 D. Praying
 E. Meeting with the church

Text

The Bible is a wonderful book. It tells us of God's full salvation. It also tells us how we can receive this salvation and grow into it fully. We will call our initial receiving of this salvation the initial stage. The way we receive salvation in this stage is through hearing the word of the faith, repenting and believing. We will call our going on in this salvation the progressing stage. We progress in our salvation by enjoying the Lord's provision and by cooperating with Him in all things.

I. THE INITIAL STAGE

One thing we should remember is that none of us is born a Christian. Being a Christian is something with a very definite beginning in our life. Romans chapter 10 verses

8b-15a and 17 tell us that, "The word is near you, in your mouth and in your heart; that is, the word of the faith which we preach, that if you confess with your mouth, Lord Jesus, and believe in your heart that God has raised Him from among the dead, you shall be saved; for with the heart man believes unto righteousness, and with the mouth man confesses unto salvation. For the Scripture says, All who believe on Him shall not be put to shame. For there is no difference between Jew and Greek; for the same Lord of all is rich to all who call upon Him. For, Whoever calls upon the name of the Lord shall be saved. How then shall they call upon Him in whom they have not believed? And how shall they believe in Him of whom they have not heard? And how shall they hear without one who preaches? And how shall they preach unless they are sent?...So faith comes out of hearing, and hearing through the word of Christ."

A. Hearing the Preaching

These verses clearly show us how we are initially saved. First, someone tells you about this salvation. This is called "the word of the faith which we preach" (Rom. 10:8).

B. Repenting

This preaching causes you to change your mind about yourself and the world. Before you heard this word, you were going toward death and God's judgment like the rest of the world. Now, when you hear this word, you want to have God. You no longer want your sinful life. This experience is repentance.

C. Believing

This preaching of the word of the faith also causes you to feel that the gospel is so wonderful and that the Lord Jesus is so lovable. You have a desire to believe in Him and receive Him. This desire was not in you before the preaching. It was brought into you when the word of the faith came into you. This desire, then, is faith, and it is generated in you by the

Spirit and the Word. Now, this word of the faith is in your mouth and in your heart.

D. Confessing

The next thing to do is to confess with your mouth by calling on the name of the Lord or by praying to Him to tell Him that you want to receive Him.

E. Being Baptized

Mark 16:16 says, "He who believes and is baptized shall be saved." After believing and being baptized, you are saved.

F. The Result

In the beginning, you had no faith. At some time, you heard the gospel, the word of the faith. Through this hearing, you desired to turn away from the world and unto the Lord, believing in Him. Out of this desire, you called on Him and were baptized, then you were saved initially. The result is that you are forgiven, justified, reconciled, and regenerated to become a child of God having His divine life and nature.

II. THE PROGRESSING STAGE

The progressing stage of salvation starts right away. To be forgiven and to be born of God is only the beginning. Now, we all need to go on by cooperating with the Lord and enjoying His rich provision.

A. Confessing Our Sins

In order for the life within us to grow, we need to confess our sins to the Lord. Then, He will forgive and cleanse us; we will be able to come to Him without any barriers so that His life within us will be free to move and grow. In this way, we cooperate with Him.

B. Reading His Word

Next, we need to read His Word every day. His Word is Spirit and life. When we touch the Word through our mentality with our spirit, we get life. We study the Word to get the points of the truth into our mentality through our memory. We pray in His Word to receive its nourishment and be fed (2 Tim. 3:16; Matt. 4:4; John 6:63; 1 Pet. 2:2).

C. Calling on His Name

We also need to call on His name. When you call His name, you get His Person. He is now the life-giving Spirit. When you get His Person, you get His life. It is in this way that you can grow (Rom. 10:12-13).

D. Praying

We also need to pray. This is not to ask for things primarily, but to touch the living God in our spirit, to fellowship with Him, and to be filled with Him (1 Thes. 5:17).

E. Meeting with the Church

We need to meet with the church in our locality. The church is God's heart's desire. It is His expression and our family which cares for us and helps us to grow. The church satisfies God and nourishes man (1 Tim. 3:15; Eph. 2:19; Heb. 10:25).

In our daily life, we need to turn to the Lord, pray to Him, and call on His name. When trouble comes, turn to Him. When there is no trouble, turn to Him then, too. He may say that you have lied. Confess that sin to Him. He may say that you are sloppy. Confess your shortcomings to Him. In these ways, you will grow up normally and receive His salvation in full.

Questions

1. Briefly explain the initial and progressing stages of our salvation.

2. Why does regeneration belong to the initial stage?

3. Describe how we can receive salvation initially. List each important step found in Romans 10.

4. What provisions has the Lord given us to grow and to go on in the progressing stage of salvation?

Further Reference

See Compendium of God's Full Salvation (LSM),
Chapter 21.

or

1. The Parts of Man (Lee/LSM), pp. 5-7, 10, 16-17, 35-36.
2. Life-study of First Peter (Lee/LSM), pp. 56-60.

Lesson Twenty-One

THE ASSURANCE AND SECURITY OF SALVATION

Scripture Reading

Heb. 6:18; Psa. 119:89; John 3:16; Acts 10:43;
1 John 5:10; Rom. 8:16; 1 John 3:14; Eph. 1:4-5;
Rom. 1:16-17; John 10:28

Outline

I. Assurance of salvation
   A. According to the Word of God
   B. According to the witness of the Holy Spirit
   C. According to the experience of life
II. Security of salvation
   A. By the will of God
   B. By the selection and calling of God
   C. By the righteousness of God
   D. By the life of God

Text

Are you saved if you have repented and believed in the Lord Jesus? Is your salvation real and secure? Or is it possible to lose your salvation once you have received it? Let's read a few quotes from a booklet entitled "Assurance, Security, and Joy of Salvation" to see how we are assured of our salvation.

I. ASSURANCE OF SALVATION

A. According to the Word of God

"He who believes and is baptized shall be saved" (Mark 16:16). "For, Whoever calls upon the name of the Lord shall be saved" (Rom. 10:13). These two statements [prove that once a person believes and is baptized, calling upon the name of the Lord, he is immediately saved. This fact should be

recognized and acknowledged immediately without dependence on human feelings.]

"He who hears My word and believes Him who sent Me
has eternal life, and Will not come into judgment, but has
passed out of death into life" (John 5:24). "He who has the Son
has the life; he who does not have the Son of God does not
have the life. I write these things to you that you may know
that you have eternal life, to you who believe in the name
of the Son of God" (1 John 5:12-13). These two portions of
Scripture [prove that once a person believes in the heavenly
Father and believes into the name of the Son of God (the Lord
Jesus Christ), he has eternal life (that is, the life of God). He
will not come into judgment and perish, but has passed out of
death into life. A person is saved in this way to have the life of
God based on what the Bible says and not on his own
feelings.]

"But as many as received Him, to them He gave authority
to become children of God, to those who believe in His name:
who were born...of God" (John 1:12-13). [The Lord Jesus gives
to those who receive Him by faith, that is, to those who
believe into His name, the authority to become children of
God. This authority is the life of God, enabling those who
believe into the Lord Jesus to be born of God, that is, to be
regenerated to become children of God. This is also proven by
the words of the Bible and not determined by human feelings.

The words in the Bible are trustworthy and can never be
changed or annulled. Human feelings will fluctuate according
to mood and environment and are undependable. Since the
Bible clearly states that a person is saved upon believing in
the Lord Jesus, this fact is then established regardless of
human feeling. We should stand on the trustworthy words of
the Bible and disregard our fluctuating feelings, believing
strongly and knowing with assurance that we have been
saved.]

B. According to the Witness of the Holy Spirit

"The Spirit Himself witnesses with our spirit that we are
the children of God" (Rom. 8:16). [When we believe in the

Lord Jesus, receiving Him as our Savior, God gives His Holy Spirit to us, putting His Spirit into our spirit (Ezek. 36:27). This Holy Spirit is in us to be with us eternally (John 14:17). He witnesses in our spirit that we are the children of God, who are born of God. Every one of us who believes in the Lord likes to address God as "Abba, Father" (Rom. 8:15). It is very natural for us to address God as "Abba, Father." As we address God in this way, we feel sweet and comfortable within. This is because we are children who are born of God, with God's life, and the Spirit of God's Son has entered into us. This is the inward proof of our salvation.]

C. According to the Experience of Life

"Everyone who believes that Jesus is the Christ has been begotten of God, and everyone who loves Him who begets, loves him who has been begotten of Him" (1 John 5:1). [Once we believe that Jesus is the Christ, we are born of God. God is love (1 John 4:16), and the life of God is also the life of love. Therefore, everyone who is begotten of God loves God and loves him who has been begotten of God, him who is a brother in the Lord.]

"We know that we have passed out of death into life, because we love the brothers" (1 John 3:14). [This word states that, as believers, our love for the brothers in the Lord is a proof that we have God's eternal life. Loving the brothers in the Lord is an experience in the eternal life of God after we have believed in the Lord to be saved. There is an unexplainable joy and feeling of dearness when a saved person sees a brother in the Lord. This kind of love toward a brother in the Lord is also a proof for us to know that we have been saved. It can be called the proof of love, the proof of our experience in the life of God.

Therefore, whether it is by the definite word of the Bible, by the witnessing of the Holy Spirit in our spirit, or by our experience of love in life, we may know assuredly that we are saved. Furthermore, the salvation that we have received is an eternal salvation (Heb. 5:9). Once we have received this salvation, we shall by no means perish forever, and no one can snatch us out of the Lord's and the heavenly Father's hands (John 10:28-29).]

We are sure that we are saved by the written Word of God, the Spirit's inward witnessing, and our experience of life.

II. SECURITY OF SALVATION

God's salvation is eternal. We can never be unsaved once we have been saved. God can't change it. We can't change it, and Satan can't change it either.

A. By the Will of God

[God's eternal salvation is secured by the will of God. Ephesians 1:5 says that we have been predestinated according to God's will, and John 6:39 tells us that the Father's will is that none of those whom He has given the Son should be lost. This is the will of God concerning our salvation. God's will is more steady and stable than a rock. Although heaven and earth may be removed, God's will remains forever. It does not go up and down like an elevator.]

B. By the Selection and Calling of God

[God's salvation is secured by the selection and calling of God. He has chosen us, selected us, before the foundation of the world (Eph. 1:4). It is not we who selected Him but He who selected us (John 15:16), and His selection is not of our works but of Himself who calls (Rom. 9:11). He has not only predestinated us but also called us (Rom 8:30), not according to our works but according to His own purpose (2 Tim. 1:9). His calling is irrevocable. He will never repent of it nor regret having called us. His selection and calling have nothing to do with our works; our works can never affect them, for they are unchangeable. Both God's selection and calling, being initiated by Him, not by us, are the security of our salvation.]

C. By the Righteousness of God

[God's eternal salvation is secured by the righteousness of God which is revealed to faith (Rom. 1:16-17). For the showing forth of His righteousness, God must justify us, and He has justified us who believe in the Lord Jesus (Rom. 3:26). It is the righteous God who has justified us (Rom. 8:33). His righteousness is the foundation of His throne (Psa. 89:14, Heb.). His throne is established forever.]

D. By the Life of God

[Our salvation is eternally secured by the life of God. The Lord said, "I give to them eternal life, and they shall by no means perish forever" (John 10:28). Do you believe that the eternal life can be recalled once it has been given to us? To say that once we are saved we can be lost again means that the eternal life which has been given to us would be called back. This is altogether illogical. Once we have the eternal life, we shall never perish.]

By all these things, we can see that our salvation is eternal. It does not change with time. It does not change if we are good or bad. It does not change and it cannot change eternally.

Questions

1. Explain what the words "assurance" and "security" mean.

2. What does it mean to say that our salvation is eternally secure?

3. Give the three things which assure us that we are saved.

4. Why is our salvation secured by the will of God?

Quoted Portions

1. Life Lessons (Lee/LSM), pp. 6-9.

2. Life-study of Hebrews (Lee/LSM), pp. 160-162.

Further Reference

See Compendium of God's Full Salvation (LSM), Chapter 25.

or

1. Gospel Outlines (Lee/LSM), p. 350.

2. The Normal Christian Faith (Nee/LSM), pp. 143-144, 155.

3. The New Covenant (Nee/LSM), pp. 58-61.

4. Life-study of Ephesians (Lee/LSM), pp. 39-40, 544-545.

5. Life-study of First Corinthians (Lee/LSM), pp. 22-23.

6. Life-study of Hebrews (Lee/LSM), pp. 135-136, 160-163, 312-313.

7. Life-study of Romans (Lee/LSM), pp. 55-56, 163, 255-257, 609-612.

8. What is Regeneration? (Lee/LSM), p. 20.

9. Life-study of Exodus (Lee/LSM), p. 712.

10. Life-study of Genesis (Lee/LSM), pp. 1459-1460.

11. Life-study of John (Lee/LSM), pp. 267-268.

Lesson Twenty-Two

THREE STAGES OF SALVATION

Scripture Reading

Heb. 2:3a; 12:1; Acts 26:19; 1 Cor. 9:24; Phil. 3:12-14;
2 Tim. 4:7-8; Rev. 22:12

Outline

I. The initial stage
II. The progressing stage
III. The completing stage
    A. Our body transfigured
    B. Expressing and representing God
    C. The way to arrive

Text

By now you must have noticed that God's full salvation is not once and for all. His salvation is in three stages according to our experience of life. Man is of three parts: spirit, soul and body. God's salvation is of three stages to fully save this three-part man.

I. THE INITIAL STAGE

The first stage of salvation is the initial stage. This stage saves our spirit. God has done this firstly by His death on the cross to take care of our objective problem before God. Second, as the life-giving Spirit, He has regenerated us in our spirit. This stage includes redemption, forgiveness of sins, cleansing of sins, justification and reconciliation. The result is regeneration. This is the beginning of the Christian life.

II. THE PROGRESSING STAGE

The second stage is the progressing stage. This stage saves us in our soul. Although God is now in our human spirit through regeneration, our soul is still full of Satan's nature.

We think evil thoughts. We lie and hate others. We are jealous and full of our own opinions. We love what God hates and hate what God loves. We are evil, we are sin, and even in a certain sense, we are Satan. But, we are also Christians who have received the divine life into us. In this stage, God deals with our evil soul. Regeneration only puts Christ into our spirit. We need to allow Christ to spread into our soul day by day. This will take our entire lifetime. By opening to Him, by praying and by confessing our sins, we allow Him to spread in us. This spreading is our sanctification. In this way, He deposits His holy nature into our soul from our spirit. At the same time He transforms us from an old man to a new man, from being full of the satanic life to being full of God.

III. THE COMPLETING STAGE

The third stage is the completing stage. In this stage our body is saved and God's full salvation reaches its climax. It is the result of the second stage. Leaving the starting block in the race is the initial stage. Running the course is the progressing stage. Crossing the finish line is the completing stage. You cannot cross the finish line unless you have started and progressed in the course of the race. The faster you progress, the earlier you will complete the race.

A. Our Body Transfigured

This stage is glorious. It finally solves all our problems and consummates God's eternal purpose. In this stage, our body is conformed to the body of the Lord's glory. Our body is transfigured, glorified. We inherit God's kingdom to reign with Christ as co-kings and obtain the topmost enjoyment of the Lord.

B. Expressing and Representing God

By this stage, our spirit will be full of life due to regeneration. Our soul will be full of Christ due to sanctification and transformation. We will think the way God thinks. We will love what God loves and hate what He hates. Our will will always choose what God would choose, and our body will be full of the glory of the Lord. Then we will fully be sons of God, full of God's life, expressing God and representing Him eternally. Through all of this process, we will be built together as the glorious church, the New Jerusalem. Hallelujah! God will be fully satisfied and we will be fully saved!

C. The Way to Arrive

We can only arrive at this stage by being initially saved and then by being sanctified and transformed. Brothers and sisters, don't you want to arrive at the third stage? If you do, then go on to enjoy Him as the Spirit and the Word. Then, cooperate with Him daily. Allow Him to spread in you by always following His leading within you and by confessing your sins and shortcomings to Him. In these ways, you will go on from the initial stage of your salvation through the progressive stage, and you will enter into the full enjoyment of your salvation in the completing stage.

Questions

1. Explain the differences between the three different stages of salvation.

2. God's salvation is not once for all but with a beginning, a continuation or a progression, and a climax. Briefly describe and explain each stage of salvation.

3. List the three stages of salvation as they related to the three parts of man in God's salvation.

Further Reference

See Compendium of God's Full Salvation (LSM), Chapter 20 and 26.

or

1. Life-study of Matthew (Lee/LSM), p. 587.

2. Life-study of Romans (Lee/LSM), pp. 13, 252-254, 273-275, 453-454, 494-495, 556, 565-566.

3. Life-study of Colossians (Lee/LSM), pp. 245-246, 525-526.

4. Life-study of Second Corinthians (Lee/LSM), pp. 33-34, 105-106, 524, 526-529.

5. Life-study of Genesis (Lee/LSM), pp. 124-125.

6. The Kingdom (Lee/LSM), p. 390.

7. Life-study of Hebrews (Lee/LSM), pp. 104-105, 136-137, 230-231, 263-264, 422-423.

8. Life-study of Ephesians (Lee/LSM), pp. 168, 314-315, 434, 480-481, 551-552.

9. Life-study of John (Lee/LSM), pp. 67-68, 218, 383, 407-409, 458, 491, 565-567.

10. The Divine Dispensing of the Divine Trinity (Lee/LSM), pp. 223, 234.

11. The Spirit and Body (Lee/LSM), p. 25.

12. Life-study of Philippians (Lee/LSM), pp. 86, 97-98, 328, 338, 340-342, 356-357, 364, 383.

13. Life-study of Revelation (Lee/LSM), p. 428.

14. Young People's Training (Lee/LSM), pp. 179-180.

15. Life-study of First Peter (Lee/LSM), pp. 92, 129, 134, 303-305.

16. Life-study of Exodus (Lee/LSM), pp. 407, 550, 888-889.

17. The Kernel of the Bible (Lee/LSM), p. 17.

18. Life-study of First Corinthians (Lee/LSM), pp. 418, 523-524.

19. Experiencing Christ as the Offerings for the Church Meetings (Lee/LSM), pp. 25-26, 52.

20. Life Messages, vol. 1 (Lee/LSM), p. 256.

21. Concerning the Triune God, the Father, the Son, and the Spirit (Lee/LSM), pp. 1-5.

22. The Stream (Lee/LSM), vol. 4, no. 2, p. 13.

23. Truth Messages (Lee/LSM), pp. 9-10, 16-18.

24. Perfecting Training (Lee/LSM), pp. 341-343, 347-350.

25. Experience of Christ (Lee/LSM), pp. 45-46.

26. The Experience of Life (Lee/LSM), pp. 151-152, 244.

27. The Economy of God (Lee/LSM), pp. 73, 90-93.

28. The Parts of Man (Lee/LSM), pp. 21-22, 33.

29. Life-study of Galatians (Lee/LSM), pp. 242, 251-252.

30. Life-study of Second Peter (Lee/LSM), pp. 27-28, 45.

Lesson Twenty-Three

REWARD AND PUNISHMENT

Scripture Reading

Matt. 25:14-30; 1 Cor. 3:10-15; 2 Cor. 5:10

Outline

I. For the believers
II. Reward for the faithful and punishment for the lazy

Text

God's salvation is not something we receive once and for all. Rather, it is a lifelong matter which the Apostle Paul and other writers in the Bible have likened to running a race. God does not want His children to be lazy and sloppy in developing the salvation that they have been given. In His wisdom He has prepared both a reward for His faithful and diligent children and a punishment for his lazy and disobedient ones. In this lesson, we want to show in brief how God has planned for this. By understanding this matter, you will be helped to not neglect the salvation you have received and you will be encouraged to pursue your full salvation and the reward which awaits you.

In the Bible, there are many passages which speak about the reward and punishment of the believers. One of the clearest is in Matthew 25:14-30. Let us read that passage now.

I. FOR THE BELIEVERS

Many people today do not believe that God will punish those believers who have been lazy and unprofitable to the Lord in this life. They say that God is too loving and merciful to do that to any of His children. However, in this passage it is more than clear that some of the Lord's servants, who must be His believers, will suffer a severe punishment from the Lord when He returns. Yes, the Lord is loving and merciful

and He will never allow one of His saved children to be lost in
the lake of fire. His salvation assures us all that none of His
believers will ever suffer the punishment which the unbeliev-
ers will suffer. But, in His wisdom, God knew that if He did
not prepare a reward as an incentive and a punishment as a
warning, few of His children would reach His goal.

In the passage in Matthew, the Lord clearly rewards His
servants for profiting Him and punishes those who do not.
This is the proper, biblical understanding.

II. REWARD FOR THE FAITHFUL
AND PUNISHMENT FOR THE LAZY

According to the Bible, God will reward some of His believers who have been faithful and diligent, and He will punish
those who have not. This is biblical, logical and fair. Would it
be fair and reasonable for the poorest students in your school
to be rewarded with a banquet and a gift of money along with
those students who studied diligently and received the high-
est grades? Would it be fair for a believer who had never
progressed in his salvation due to laziness and sinfulness to
be rewarded in the same way as the Apostle Paul? No, of
course not. It would be unfair to the diligent. The Bible also
teaches us differently.

Today, we are God's children through regeneration. How
are we progressing? Are we being sanctified and transformed
every day? Are we growing in life? Are we serving Him as a
faithful servant in the church life? The Bible tells us clearly
that at His second coming, the Lord will come to firstly judge
all of His believers. He will reward or punish them according
to their work. Then He will judge the world and all its people.
Those who have been faithful will be ushered into the kingdom and a wedding feast to enjoy Christ for a thousand years.
The unfaithful ones will suffer His punishment by being cast
into outer darkness away from the Lord's presence.

By growing in the Lord's life and by faithfully serving
Him today, we may be those whom the Lord rewards with the
thousand-year kingdom and the wedding feast. Let us be
encouraged by this reward and warned by the fact that we

could suffer a punishment. Keeping these things in mind, we will be greatly helped to go on with the Lord in His full salvation.

Questions

1. Explain the passage in Matthew showing that the Lord will both reward and punish His believers.

2. Why is it wise for the Lord to prepare a reward or punishment for His children?

3. What punishment will the unfaithful believers receive?

4. What reward will the faithful receive?

5. How does this matter show not only the Lord's love and grace but His wisdom as well?

Further Reference

See Compendium of God's Full Salvation (LSM), Chapter 29.

or

1. The Kingdom (Lee/LSM), pp. 337, 340-342, 532-534, 536-537, 539-540.

2. Life-study of Hebrews (Lee/LSM), pp. 159-160, 174-179, 181, 228-229, 246, 256.

3. Life-study of Matthew (Lee/LSM), pp. 765-768.

4. The Exercise of the Kingdom for the Building of the Church (Lee/LSM), pp. 41, 57-58.

5. Life-study of First Corinthians (Lee/LSM), pp. 252-253.

Lesson Twenty-Four

CONCLUSION

Scripture Reading

Eph. 1:10, 4-5; Rom. 5:18-19, 10; 8:29; Rev. 22:1-5

Outline

I. God purposed
II. God selected
III. God created and Satan corrupted
IV. God's salvation
V. In eternity future

Text

I. GOD PURPOSED

In eternity past, God had a purpose according to the good pleasure of His will. This purpose was to have a group of people, a corporate man, filled up with Himself as life. This corporate man would have His image to express Him and His dominion to represent Him and to rule over His enemy. In time, this corporate man is just the church, God's heart's desire. In eternity future, it will be the New Jerusalem. This is what He has always been after. Only this will make Him happy. His economy is just to carry out this purpose by dispensing Himself into man.

II. GOD SELECTED

Before He created the universe, He chose and predestinated some men to be part of this corporate man. These chosen ones would become His sons, full of His life to express Him and to inherit all He is.

III. GOD CREATED AND SATAN CORRUPTED

In time, He created the heavens, the earth, and all of

mankind in one man named Adam. This man was to be filled with God as life. He placed him in front of the tree of life, but due to Satan's deception he chose to take the tree of knowledge instead. As a result of Adam's sinning against God, he fell under God's condemnation objectively and received the satanic nature into Him subjectively.

IV. GOD'S SALVATION

God created; Satan corrupted. Then God came in and promised to save man. He promised and prophesied in the Old Testament about the coming Savior-God. Then, in the New Testament, Jesus, the Savior-God, came and fulfilled all these promises and prophecies given by God. He was incarnated as a man, lived for thirty-three and a half years as a proper human being, and was crucified for our redemption. In this redemption, forgiveness of sins, cleansing of sins, justification and reconciliation were all included. All of man's objective problems before God were solved.

In resurrection, He became the life-giving Spirit to regenerate us in our spirit. He is now working within us to save our soul by His life, sanctifying and transforming us. For this, we need to enjoy His rich provision and be obedient to His inner leading.

In the future, when He comes again, He will redeem our sinful and fallen body to be like His glorious body. This is to be conformed fully to His image (Rom. 8:29).

V. IN ETERNITY FUTURE

Then, in eternity future, all of the chosen and redeemed people who have gone through this progressive salvation will become the New Jerusalem, the ultimate mingling of the Triune God with the tripartite man.

Hallelujah! Hallelujah! God will dwell in man and man in God for eternity. This is the ultimate goal of God, His eternal purpose. God will have finished His work according to His plan and will be fully satisfied and at rest for eternity. Amen!

Questions

1. Write a brief outline of God's full salvation, listing in appropriate order the key words you have learned.

Available at
Christian bookstores, or contact Living Stream Ministry
2431 W. La Palma Ave. • Anaheim, CA 92801
1-800-549-5164 • www.livingstream.com